Noodle Pillows

PETA MATHIAS

Noodle Pillows

A journey through
Vietnamese food and culture

ABC
Books

Acknowledgements

I am grateful to Jenny Yee for her assistance with research for this book, and to Alice Fabre for generously sharing her past with me over many bowls of pho. Thanks too to Tanah Dowdle for her companionship on part of my journey and for her photos; to Julie LeClerc for the pho photo and to Hanh Pham for proofreading the Vietnamese words.

First published in Australia by ABC Books for the
AUSTRALIAN BROADCASTING CORPORATION
GPO Box 9994 Sydney NSW 2001

Copyright © Peta Mathias

Published November 2003

The National Library of Australia Cataloguing-in-Publication entry
Mathias, Peta.
Noodle Pillows : a journey through Vietnamese food and culture.
ISBN 0 7333 1338 8.
1. Mathias, Peta - Journeys - Vietnam. 2. Cookery,
Vietnamese. 3. Vietnam - Description and travel. 4.
Vietnam - Social life and customs. I. Australian
Broadcasting Corporation. II. Title.
915.97

Design and production by **Book**NZ (www.booknz.co.nz)
Map of Vietnam by Chris O'Brien
Printed in China through Colorcraft Ltd., HK

Contents

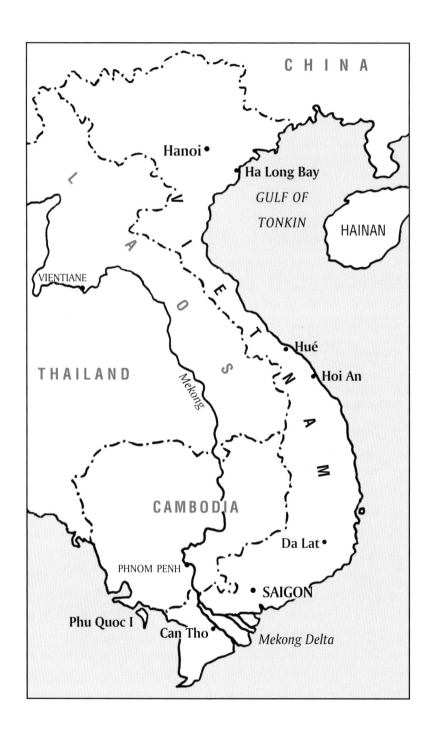

1

Hanoi

'Do you have any children?'

'No.'

'Where is your husband?'

'I'm a tragic widow.'

'How old are you?'

'I forget.'

This taxi conversation on the way from the airport to my hotel in Hanoi was not impertinence. Any person in a developing country knows that a woman without children is deserving of unlimited kindness, sympathy and open-mouthed astonishment. That I came to be in this incomprehensible situation by choice is a philosophical conundrum I wouldn't even consider burdening a young Vietnamese taxi driver with.

'Where are you staying, madame?'

'Thiên Thai Hotel, I think.'

'Why you go there, madame? Is no good. You want go old quarter. All tourist want go old quarter. I take you somewhere very good.'

'Okay'.

'Okay?'

'Yeah okay. I'm in your hands.'

I was in Vietnam for the first time in my life, on the trail of pho – that simple but complex soup which is Vietnam in a bowl, heaven in a spoon, culture in a sip. The word pho is a bastardisation of the French word feu, and is pronounced the same. This beef noodle soup is legendary, not only in the lives of the Vietnamese but also in my own life. I first tasted pho in Paris in the 1980s. I had a restaurant in the 5th arrondissement and not far from it in the 13th was a tiny, narrow, hole-in-the-wall pho restaurant run by a beautiful, older Vietnamese woman we all called Madame Pho. She was the size of a chopstick, had long black hair in a bun at the base of her neck and wore traditional dress or ao dai (pronounced 'ao yai'). Madame Pho did a few other simple dishes but everyone who knew, which included the best chefs in Paris, came for her pho. It cost next to nothing, there were four tables and you had to wait for ages to get served. At the back was her primitive kitchen which, I came to realise, was a direct replica of the pavement food stalls I found all over Vietnam. It contained two burners, one for the big pot of broth and one for the pot of water in which to heat the rice noodles. Madame Pho's broth was very clear and fragrant and the raw beef was sliced razor-thin into the soup at the last moment so it came to you still rare. Her herbs were always plentiful and crisp and every bowl of soup she served was a work of art. I had so many good memories of that pho, the friends I shared it with over 10 years of summer days in Paris, that two decades later I decided to wander through Vietnam to try and recapture the pho of my dreams.

I have travelled in countries whose citizens are spectacularly unattached to driving rules (southern India comes to mind) but driving from the Hanoi airport to the Continental Hotel taught me within half an hour that in Vietnam it is best to 'be at one with the universe' because you could meet your maker any time in the next three seconds. On the road are cars, trucks, bicycles, motor scooters, cyclos (three-wheel bicycles I'll describe in more detail later), peasants and animals. Everybody drives fast and anywhere on the road that they feel like. There's a left side and a right side but the distinction is merely philosophical, not physical. You double and sometimes triple overtake and toot your horn continuously, not in warning but to let the other lunatics know you're there. It's basically a battle of nerves, with the same rules as 'chicken', but the Vietnamese are quite calm and quiet about it. At the last second, vehicular contact is avoided, sometimes by an inch. In the back seat, all air-conditioned, tinted windows and leather seats, you, the passenger, have a sphincter tighter than you dreamed possible. It doesn't, however, do to cross the Vietnamese, as various invaders over the centuries have found out. If you make a mistake in this death dance they call driving, you might not live to tell the story. One day I saw a well-dressed man slam his motor bike to a stop and slap a peasant on a rickety old honda (in Vietnam honda means motor cycle) hard across the head. He then got off his machine, kick-boxed this unfortunate young man in the back and continued punching him in the head. The young man took it passively without defending himself. I realised then that the class system was alive and well in Vietnam.

We drove through ramshackle towns, ploughing into street markets, sending chickens and people flying, flew past bright green rice paddies in the distance on either side of the highway and passed under bridges where destitute people had set up camp. The Vietnamese seemed to be very social beings. Even under the bridges, they had set up tables and chairs for drink parties and even if you had only one thing to sell, you put it on a filthy table and hawked it. If the taxi stopped for any length of time, people just stood and stared at you in the back seat as if you were a prize pig. The driver chatted non-stop, kindly pointing out the dog restaurants occupying a long row in a village. These are not places where dogs eat; they are places where people eat dogs.

I checked into the hotel the driver took me to, turned the cold shower to drench, cracked open a beer, flipped the air-con to Iceland and wondered what to do with swollen ankles. The hotel was typically Hanoi no-star, meaning tall and thin with no lift and lots of smiling young men in white shirts, black pants and nicely combed hair. Hanoi dwellings are called tube houses because they are small at the front and go a long way back. This comes from the days when owners were taxed on the width of a house, not the length. Before I could even look out the window, I was sidetracked and delighted by the nine-page hotel information folder, elucidating the area codes for every hill village and swamp outpost in Vietnam plus every country in the world including Afghanistan, American Samoa, Liechtenstein and the Vatican City. I can tell you it costs US$4.49 a minute to call Albania from Hanoi.

The house rules sheet required customers to state the 'managing organs' (don't ask me, that's what was written) if they had 'special goods' and it was absolutely forbidden to bring in explosives, weapons, inflammable liquid, radio activity or 'tonics'. (I'm pleased to say I sneaked in the Bombay Sapphire without any mention of tonics. I later deduced they probably meant toxins.) If you did bring these things in and the hotel burned down as a result of your carelessness, you must notify the staff. As for the explosives, well, in some countries I've visited you can buy them at the market.

Back to the house rules. 'After acceptation of rooms and their equipments, customers are kindly requested not to move them free willingly. When returning the rooms (from where – Albania?) customers shall transfer them to the service staff. No strangers, raw foodstuffs, strong smell goods or animals should be happened in the rooms.' Talk about putting ideas into your head. It had never occurred to me to do anything but sleep and write but here I was fantasising about strangers and equipments and not necessarily in that order. 'No washing clothes or ironing is permitted in the room.' It didn't matter what state your knickers were in: wash them and you died. 'We are honoured to keep your valuable things in the hotel's safe box.' Finally 'after your stay at the hotel, we look forward to receiving your precious opinions in order to enable us upgrading day by its quality. We extend and wish the honoured guest a good holiday and thank you for your coming.' The extraordinary thing about this bossy, linguistic fantasy was that the hotel staff were exactly the opposite – relaxed and smiling. Nothing was ever too much trouble. I felt I could have rearranged the equipments, stored my nuclear warheads and had a party of strangers in my bathroom without so much as the flutter of an eyelash.

Another really good thing about Vietnamese hotel rooms, aside from the house rules, is the television. All foreign shows, whether they be American, Chinese or Albanian, have voice-overs done by the same voice, speaking all the parts, male and female. This is most bizarre after a few beers because you don't know what they're saying and, with shock, you realise it doesn't matter, which makes you wonder why you watch television in any language. You can also get CNN, which is government controlled and regurgitated a day later so you get only good news. I find this very intelligent. I would like to live in a world where I get only good news.

The Continental hotel was definitely *in* the old quarter — if I had been any more in the old quarter, I would have been in someone's dining room, stirring the pho pot. I dived out into the hot, thick, humid, tropical, northern darkness. The first thing I noticed as I walked along was that my ankles had now swollen like boiled noodles. I had this great, cool tropical look happening — white linen blouse, spotted skirt, lipstick, hair combed, foreign eyes concealing secret torridness — and then there were the oedemic ankles. True tropical adventuresses never get fat ankles because they have the brains to visit exotic locations outside the monsoon season. But I was well and truly *inside* the monsoon season and, more importantly, hungry. The way to the famous Cha Ca La Vong restaurant was charmingly lit by the kamikaze street pilots charging up and down the streets on hondas, and by the odd street light. Music was provided by the garbage collectors who rang bells to announce their arrival and I couldn't walk on the footpath because that was for motor cycles.

I'm not sure why this restaurant, La Vong, is so famous. It could be its age (over 100 years), it could be the food or it could be that respecting the ancestors pays off. As in all Vietnamese establishments, there is an altar to Buddha surrounded by flowers, incense and offerings. You sit down at an upstairs table and are immediately presented with a laminated sign announcing, 'ONLY ONE DISH IN OUR RESTAURANT — GRILLED FISH 60,000 VND. NO DRINKING'. No explosives and now no drinking — this couldn't go on. To my relief, this edict excluded beer which I smartly ordered and waited nicely for my we-only-do-fish dish.

The Vietnamese are very good at dishes where you get to play with your food, which I approve of, and this was no exception. A cluster of little plates arrived with various ingredients perched on top: Vietnamese mint, sliced spring onions, peanuts, sweet dill, cold rice vermicelli and nuoc cham. Nuoc cham is an addictive dipping sauce made from nuoc mam (fish sauce), lime juice, chilli, sugar and garlic. Then a small clay brazier (actually, it's made of sand) full of red-hot coals is placed before you, topped with a cast iron pan of sizzling little chunks of bronzed fish. In operation A you chuck the greens into the fish, stir and let sizzle briefly, meanwhile putting some vermicelli into your bowl. Operation B consists of spooning some of the fish/herb mixture onto the noodles and garnishing with the other ingredients. You keep adding to this bowl at will till it's all gone. I found the fish mixture too greasy but it tasted very good – rather like curry with strong hints of turmeric.

More interesting was the conversation I had with the French girl and her boyfriend sitting next to me. She was articulate and very pretty, with skin the colour of roasted honey and obviously partly Asian. It turned out her father was Vietnamese and it was the first time she had visited Vietnam. Like me, when I visited my mother's home in Ireland for the first time, she had no romantic illusions of root finding and emotional family reunions. However, she and her boyfriend had fallen in love with the Vietnamese people without any help from heredity and were reluctant to leave. She found her father's family generous and loving and completely accepting as if she had never been 'away'.

I awoke after a bad night of dreaming that I was sleeping balanced on two buckets. Completely drenched in sweat, in spite of the air-con, I got dressed and the exertion meant my clothes were soaked within 10 minutes. I passed on the choice in the breakfast room: tea, beer, cigarettes, fresh fruit juice, beef noodle and eggs and 'have a good taste'. The laundry I had sent out to be washed was delivered pristine and beautifully pressed, with the underwear wrapped carefully in a little bag. Following the laundry was a gentleman bearing my breakfast cup of tea and a cut mango. The

CHA CA THANG LONG
TURMERIC FRIED FISH

This doesn't taste exactly like Cha Ca La Vong because their recipe is secret but it's still pretty good. Also I've used a lot less oil.

Serves 4 to 6
250 g (8 oz) dried rice noodles
$1/_4$ cup vegetable oil
$1/_2$ cup rice flour
1 tsp powdered turmeric or 2 tsp finely chopped fresh
$1/_2$ tsp powdered ginger or 1 tsp finely chopped fresh
$1/_2$ tsp curry powder
1 kg (2 lb) firm fleshed white fish fillets cut into 2.5 cm (1 in) squares
4 spring onions cut into 5 cm (2 in) lengths and sliced in half lengthwise
$1/_2$ cup roasted, chopped peanuts
a handful of basil leaves
a handful of coriander leaves
a handful of dill, cut into 5 cm (2 in) lengths
nuoc cham dipping sauce (see recipe p. 49)

1 Soak the noodles in warm water for 15 minutes.
2 Bring a big pot of water to the boil. Place the noodles in a sieve (might have to do this in lots) and lower them into the boiling water for 15 seconds. Remove, rinse with cold water and keep aside, covered in plastic wrap.
3 Heat the oil in a heavy-based frying-pan. Mix the flour, turmeric, ginger and curry powder in a plastic bag. Put in the fish pieces and shake the bag to cover fish in flour mixture.
4 Shake excess flour off fish and fry for about 2 minutes on each side. Place on a warm platter.
5 Add a little more oil to the pan if necessary, raise the heat to very high and throw in spring onions, peanuts and herbs. Stir-fry for about 30 seconds and place around the fish on the platter.

To serve: Put some rice noodles on your plate and top with some fish and herbs. Spoon nuoc cham over and keep adding more noodles and more fish till you are full and happy.

glistening fruit was ripe and exploding with luscious flavour. It was only 7 a.m. but as I looked down from my balcony people were already sitting down to footpath 'picnics' of pho or chao, a sort of rice porridge containing pieces of seafood or pork. A girl went past balancing a huge basket of golden baguettes. Madame Meat had set up her plank of wood low to the ground with various cuts of meat on display. There's no refrigeration and never any flies.

Down in the street, I didn't walk a metre before I saw something to eat. You could spend all day eating in this wonderland of fresh instant food. Try to imagine just sitting down on a low stool at a small table on the pavement and saying to a long-haired, smiling woman, 'I want that.' She answered in Vietnamese, explaining what it was and giggling. I stayed sitting and smiled to make it clear I really did want to try the white junkety stuff in her bucket. She placed some ice cubes in the bottom of a little bowl, on top of which was spooned the junket, on top of which was sprinkled jasmine water with jasmine flowers floating in it. It was absolutely delicious and I later found out it was made from tofu. The Vietnamese are in love with ice, introduced to them by the French. They drag huge lumps of it around the streets to sell and then bang off a bit when needed. Just the sight of it was supposed to give me the runs but I soon gave up being careful and ate and drank everything that was given to me, with very little mishap.

Another metre down the pavement and I was at it again. I recognised the big pot immediately as the thing I had come to Vietnam for – pho. I sat down on a stool and watched as the squatting woman heated a sieve full of white rice noodles in a pot of boiling water and placed them in a bowl. From her poetic display of ingredients she plucked some sliced onions, shavings of fresh ginger, some rau que or Thai basil (lemon/aniseed-flavoured), some rau mui or coriander and some bean sprouts and plopped them on top. Lastly thin slices of beef went on and the lot was covered with broth from the big pot. She handed it to me with chopsticks and a spoon and indicated the sauces. I added lots of coriander, lime juice and chilli sauce and the sweat poured out of me. She and her friends sat on their haunches, watched me intently and moved the fan closer. As my broth went down, she topped it up and demonstrated how to hold the spoon in my left hand and the chopsticks in the right, shovelling noodles in and slurping at the same time.

My first pho in Vietnam was good but not as I remembered it from Paris. The broth of my pavement feast lacked flavour and the beef was not raw; it was obviously thinly sliced well-cooked stewing beef from the stock. She dropped little spoonfuls of meat paste into the broth to create tiny dumplings, which she also gave me to taste. She showed me what to do with the bowl of kumquats the size of cherries. You cut them in half, dip them in salt and suck. The result is a smashing little explosion in your mouth.

In Vietnam's long history, it was the beef introduced by the Mongol herdsmen, who turned up in the north in the 10th century, which led to the invention of a beef broth with noodles in it. The French called this soup pot au feu annamite (annamite is the old word for Vietnamese and pot au feu means pot on the fire) and improved the stock by putting lots of bones in it and it was they who asked for the beef to be served rare. Arguably it is also the froggies who jazzed this soup up with the addition of herbs and spring onions but the other additives like nuoc mam, chillies, lime juice and bean sprouts are clearly Vietnamese. The north is famous for its huge beef farms and most of their classic dishes revolve around this meat, most spectacularly Bo Bay Mon beef, in which you are served seven different beef dishes in one meal.

Hanoi is an ancient city dating back to the Neolithic period. It used to be called Dong Kinh, which was bastardised to Tonkin by the Europeans in the 18th century. The old streets all have the names of the guilds of the trade in which they originally specialised – Pho Hang Gai or Silk Street, Bat Dan or Wooden Bowl Street, Thuoc Bac or Herbal Medicine Street. Walking through the old quarter, one is assailed good-humouredly but relentlessly by the sellers of cosmetics, sunglasses, T-shirts, jewellery and silk sleeping bags and it seems you spend your whole day saying, 'No, thank you.' A ravishing brown girl laden with a pyramid of non bai tho or conical hats saw me standing like a dope in the 32°C sun, all red hair and fair skin, begging the melanoma god to take me. She crossed the road and put a hat on me, tying the purple ribbon under my chin. These hats are surprisingly light and not at all cumbersome to wear so I bought one gratefully, then stepped into the Little Hanoi Café for the very special way coffee is made in this country.

Coffee Vietnamese style sounds horrendous but I found it really good. It's strong and, bizarrely, made with condensed milk. They use very cute individual drippers which are placed on top of the cup already containing the condensed milk. Ground coffee is placed in the first chamber, the filter is placed on top and boiling water poured in. If you want an iced coffee, they just plop a few ice-cubes in the cup and follow the same method. It was the French who introduced Vietnam to coffee, condensed milk, coffee filters – and ice, for that matter. Vietnamese-grown coffee – the best Arabica beans are from the central highlands in the area of Ban Me Thuot – is of very high quality. Unfortunately, the coffee beans are often roasted in butter so taste of vanilla, but if you ask, you can buy them natural. In spite of what the guidebooks say, any other kind of coffee made in Western-style cafés is rubbish – cappuccinos and espressos are dire even when the correct machines are used. Ducking into cafés and bars not only replenishes some of the lost liquids but gives you a break from the racket. The Vietnamese love noise. They toot loudly all day long and most of the night, roar around on noisy hondas, play loud radios, ring bells, enjoy but ignore live propaganda broadcasts and yoo-hoo to you everywhere you go.

While I was combing the crowded old quarter streets I came across a hotel I thought I would like better than the Continental. The rooms were lighter and had a proper view of the street from the balcony. I moved house, to the utter devastation of my Continental friends. My new hotel, Classic Street (great title for a movie) on Hang Be Street, also had very friendly staff. One man was so keen to learn English, he repeated everything I said. I would say, 'I'm here to write a book on Vietnamese food', and he would say softly and intently, 'Ah, I am here to write a book on Vietnamese food.' Outside my first-floor door was an inner courtyard and outside my french doors on the other side of the room was a balcony opening to the street. This became my cinema, my microcosm of Hanoi life which, like the weather, changed every hour. Between these two openings, I felt as though I was living in a little tower. When I awoke the next morning it was raining but this changes nothing in Hanoi; it just means the transparent blue raincoats go on, and a few hats and umbrellas appear. The upside of the rain is that the temperature goes down markedly.

Every morning I had pho for breakfast, either at the little stand across the road or the hotel would make me some and bring it up to my room. The hotel pho was very simple and I always had to ask for nuoc mam and extra herbs. I noticed that pho is normally served for breakfast but you can get it on the street all day. From my balcony I could see straight into the tall, skinny houses across the street – ornate shuttered balconies displaying washing and flowering vines, birds singing in the trees, someone practising scales on the piano, fans whirring and a toddler standing at a window staring at me. A woman went past balancing a huge load on her head, no hands. Across the street another woman spent all day in front of a basket of tiny silver fish, another squatted before her limes, another presided over a basket of plucked chickens. Mountains of neatly arranged flowers sailed by on bicycles. No one ever looked tired or stressed and they could sleep anywhere in any position.

The women work very hard and the men appear to do nothing much but drink and sit around reading the paper and watching women work. According to my discussion with the hotel clerk, this is entirely normal because men are superior and need a lot of time to think. Women seem to be trained from birth to serve everyone – their men, their mothers-in-law, their children, their employers. It seems to me the Vietnamese economy will rise and conquer on the backs of women. Poor women and girls don't have much status or many rights except as workhorses and because they do most of the housework and childcare on top of the all-day jobs, they have no time for leisure, education or social and cultural activities. Most of women's work is unpaid and when they are paid, they receive 70 per cent of the hourly wage of men, even if the job is exactly the same. Women are overwhelmingly concentrated in lower skilled professions and are less likely to be found in senior management positions. It's hard for a woman to get a loan, for example, because the joint property is usually in the husband's name. If poor girls get to primary school they're lucky and they hardly ever get to secondary school. If anyone's to be given a chance in the family, it'll be the boys. This gender inequality is not only unfair but also short-sighted, since it keeps women poor and uneducated when they could be contributing a lot more to the economy.

Across the road from the hotel was one of the entrances to the T-shaped flower market which starts off selling flowers but quickly becomes a food and cooking market. The best food in Hanoi is probably on the street and this market was a sizzling wonderworld of gourmet treats. Catfish, sea bream, sea bass, red snapper, flounder and tuna lay in big plastic bowls of water or on slabs. When a customer bought one it was yanked out of the water, banged on the head and gutted and filleted right there and then. Trussed crabs, squid, clams, snails and eels were busily trying to escape from their baskets. The fabulously mouth-watering prawns came in every size from microscopic ones wiggling in a big pile to gigantic tiger ones you just wanted to sink your teeth into like a wild cat. Birds in cages were singing their hearts out but the pigeons, quails and chickens squashed into larger cages had a less musical future. The girl opened the cage, grabbed one which shrieked knowingly, bent its neck back and stuck it in the gullet with her sharp knife. It went to heaven swiftly, was plucked, washed, emptied and in your pho ga (chicken pho) before it even realised its beak was missing.

An old woman with betel-stained black teeth was checking her duck eggs for signs of life, looking at them one by one through a viewfinder made of rolled-up newspaper. In the city, one rarely sees these black teeth nowadays but there was a time when most rural women chewed betel leaves the way Americans chew tobacco and Bolivians chew coca. Betel is the round, large, crinkled, peppery leaf of the pepper vine, also used in soups, to wrap food and as decoration on plates. It has a herbal fragrance but the inevitable end result is bad and permanent staining of the teeth. I was told it was a natural antidote to dental caries but, as someone else said, how would you know if the teeth were rotten or not? It was lunchtime for me (1 p.m.) but nap time for the stall holders who normally ate around 11 a.m. because they had been up since 5 a.m. Everywhere women slept where they worked – on stools, lying on a plank in the middle of the fish, slumped on the noodles, up against a wall with their hat pulled down. People's homes opened right onto the street and they were all watching soap operas, enthralled and spellbound.

I decided to try some upmarket Hanoi cooking so called my contact, executive chef Donald Berger at the Press Club. The club, opposite the Sofitel Metropole Hotel in central Hanoi, has only been open a few years and Donald is regarded as one of the best chefs in Hanoi, his dishes rivalling any to be found on the menu in New York or London. The interesting thing about Hanoi is the ex-pat scene. You go to the bars and restaurants they frequent and you would never know you were in Vietnam. The Press Club is in this category, complete with English bookshop, café, delicatessen serving French pastries, classy library bar, terrace bar with music and fine dining restaurant where the staff dip every plate and every piece of cutlery in hot water and polish them before the service. Donald is a softly spoken, nice-looking Canadian, married to a Thai woman and in love with Vietnamese food. In his opinion, pho is the best dish in the Vietnamese repertoire and he will go a long way to get a good one. He trained in Canada, has worked internationally and sources his produce from all over the world. A lot of the vegetables come from Da Lat in the central highlands, the garden of Vietnam; the foie gras is produced by a farmer in Shanghai he has worked with for several years; the beluga caviar comes from China; 20 kilos of buffalo mozzarella is flown in twice weekly from outside Rome; the beef and lamb come from the United States. Who wouldn't die for a budget like that?

I dragged out my wrinkled best dress which I don't believe Comme des Garçons designed for schlepping around Hanoi slums, but may have thought up with the Press Club in mind, and settled myself in to sip the glass of Mumms Donald had sent to my table. From then on, I had trouble keeping up with the stream of plates I was sent. Donald came out between each dish to enthuse with me and tell me where it all came from and how he had cooked it. He loves looking after his customers and gave personal attention to almost every table, which I found extraordinary in a restaurant of this calibre. There isn't a pretentious bone in this man's body and he has trained his Vietnamese staff to very high standards. Not that it's hard to do – the Vietnamese are naturally sensitive cooks who are willing to learn. And they have the advantage of being born in a country whose cuisine was formed by the two greatest gastronomic cultures in the world – Chinese and French.

A spoon of tender, white mozzarella topped with salty, black caviar and drizzled with extra virgin Italian olive oil was placed before me. This was followed by something I had mentioned to Donald as being my dream food, the meal I would request before they threw the switch. Foie gras. We all know that foie gras is desperately rich with an incomparable taste and that we eat very little of it at a sitting if we have any sort of relationship with our livers. Two large, thick slices of seared, fattened, goose liver stared up at me – I almost had a crise de foie just looking at it. Donald laughed and said, 'I told the kitchen to give you just a little taste.' I managed to eat half of it, helped by the salutary digestive properties of a late harvest gewürztraminer riesling.

Meanwhile, just through the lacquered, shuttered doors, it was tapas night in the bar with a jazz band. Feeling absolutely no urgency to waste my time among Western tourists with bad accents and loud shirts, I set myself to sampling a carpaccio of very pale Tonkin sea tuna topped with julienned cu dau or jicama, a root vegetable tasting a bit like a cross between apple and turnip. This was seriously classy world food with a definite Asian pizzaz adding cleanness and lightness without sacrificing depth. The restaurant was a very pleasant place to be in too, with its elegant, contemporary Asian decor. Interestingly, in all the French international style restaurants I ate in Vietnam, the clientele were almost exclusively

Thit Lon Nuong Ong Tre
Marinated Pork Grilled in Bamboo

Serves 6

1 kg (2 lb) pork shoulder, sliced
6 tbsp caramel – recipe overleaf
2 tbsp nuoc mam
40 g (2 oz) chopped shallots
80 g (3 oz) sliced spring onions
thumb-sized piece of fresh ginger, chopped
1 chilli, chopped
2 bamboo tubes 25 cm (10 in) long, 7 cm (3 in) in diameter
2 large banana leaves, washed
kitchen string
fresh coriander for garnish
nuoc mam

1 Marinate pork with caramel, nuoc mam, shallots, spring onions, ginger and chilli for half an hour.
2 Cut the bamboo in half lengthwise and clean. Cut 4 pieces of banana leaf to fit the halves and layer the bamboo with them.
3 Divide the pork mixture into the 4 pieces of bamboo, put the halves together and tie up with string.
4 Grill on a charcoal fire for 10 minutes on each side.

To serve: Serve with rice (see recipe p. 145). Place the opened bamboo halves on the table, garnish the meat with some coriander and allow guests to help themselves. Have a bottle of nuoc mam handy in case there are any addicts.

Alternative Method of Cooking

Lay a bed of spring onions on a folding grill, place the pork on top, cover with more spring onions, close the grill and place on an oven tray to catch drips. Cook under the oven grill at 250°C (480°F) for 10 minutes each side. To eat, discard the spring onions and proceed as above. The pork will be infused with the taste of spring onions, but not overwhelmed by it, and it smells fantastic as you lift them off.

Vietnamese Caramel

3 tbsp sugar
1 tbsp thick soy sauce
3 tbsp nuoc mam
freshly ground black pepper

1 Put the sugar and 2 tbsp water in a heavy-based pot and boil on a medium heat for about 10 minutes until the sugar melts and turns thick and golden.
2 Remove from the heat and add $1/3$ cup of water, soy sauce, nuoc mam and 4 good turns of the peppermill.
3 On a low heat, simmer for another 5–10 minutes till the caramel thickens a bit. This should make 6 tbsp of caramel. Cool completely before using because if you put cold meat into a hot caramel, the caramel will harden and you will burst into tears.

French, ex-pats or foreigners of some description. Although the French were there for 100 years, the 'fusion' of Vietnamese and French styles is fairly minimal – maybe 20 dishes all together – when you consider there are at least 500 traditional Vietnamese recipes. You don't very often see Vietnamese in these restaurants; they prefer their own cuisine. I feel bound to tell you that there are some very handsome men in Vietnam – the north is supposedly famous for them – and a number of them, I'm happy to say, were in this restaurant serving me. They have beautiful brown skin, chiselled jaws, high cheek bones and, like the women, good posture and finely shaped bodies. The pièce de resistance was Annamese sea bream, a rather tender fish served on a bed of cai tau or mustard greens. Mustard greens look a bit like lettuce but have a sharp clean taste and these combined nicely with the mellow flavour of a mandarin and coriander butter sauce. Tiny shards of sweet buoi or pomelo (like huge grapefruit) were rained on top. To me this was the best dish I tasted there because it really symbolised Donald's approach and it worked structurally – the method was classic French but the ingredients were Vietnamese.

As I left the Press Club Donald introduced me to my very own honda om driver and this gentleman stayed on call for me throughout my time in Hanoi. Honda means motor cycle and om means hug, so the passenger wraps their arms around the driver to stay on. All I had to do was call him up on his cellphone from my cellphone and he would be there in a flash to pick me up. You can also get a ride on a cyclo or pedal-operated tricycle with an attached seat for one or two passengers. The advantage of this form of transport is you're not adding to the city's pollution and it's slow and romantic (unless someone drives into you). Travelling by honda om is a bit more scary as they go very fast but this man had been recommended because he was moderate and trustworthy. Normally he wore a shirt, pants and thongs and in the rain this outfit was enhanced with a khaki raincoat and safari hat. Unlike the cyclo cowboys, he was reserved and chivalrous and, if he was unable to stop outside, always escorted me across the road to my destination. If I missed calling him for a few days, he greeted me with unabashed joy when I reappeared.

Another evening I tried Club Opera, an expensive Vietnamese restaurant right next door to the Press Club. The decor was entirely European with white linen tablecloths and bunches of fresh pink roses on every table. Goddesses with perfect, slim figures floated around in salmon pink ao dais, the wine list included a bottle of Mersault Louis Jadot '97, a mere snip at US$135, and across the room a loud foreign businessman was doing a deal with two Englishmen in a very annoying, staccato accent. He sounded like a Russian machine gun talking to Chelsea humming birds. He would never have got into the Continental – one sentence and they would have shown him the explosives clause. I had to eat as quickly as possible so I could get out of there before I made a slingshot of my hair tie and sent some wet kim chi his way. Before breaking point I did manage to stuff in some banh goi crispy pillow cakes and a line-up of vit chien sot quit sliced duck breast with mandarin sauce. The former were stuffed with pork and glass noodles and deep-fried till they blew up like little pillows. It was like eating floating fragments of crispness.

The Sofitel Metropole is one of the best hotels in Hanoi. I don't see the point in protecting yourself from a culture by staying in a luxurious hotel which may be anywhere in the world, but that may be jealousy. How can the inhabitants of five-star hotels possibly know anything of the life I experienced below my Classic Street hotel terrace. As the saying goes, if you're not on the edge then you're taking up too much room. In the old quarter, you get the picture, for better or for worse. However, I forgave the Metropole their luxuriousness long enough to enjoy a few afternoon teas with tiny French pastries and to attend one of their famous cooking classes. I turned up at 10 a.m. sharp and, of course, no one else did. It was raining and I was decked out in my Vietnamese monsoon look of transparent filmy raincoat with hood, big enough to fit over you and honda om, you and shopping, you and notebook.

Eventually everyone turned up and the class gathered under the capable wing of chef Madame Mai to be taken off to the 1912 (meaning 19 December) market. As a result of some nutty bureaucratic decision, this wonderful old market will soon be pulled down to build another one, so get there as soon as you can to partake in the smells, sounds, life and colour of a great Hanoi institution. The 1912 is a very tight, intense market, made even more crushed by the infernal habit of people driving right in and down the aisles on their bicycles and hondas. The authorities tried to ban this procedure but people objected as they liked the convenience of racing in, picking up the veggies and fish, running over everyone's feet and zooming off again.

I tried to take note of the dozens of herbs and greens Madame Mai was explaining and rubbing under our nostrils in the market but it was impossible in the rain and it's harder to write under a raincoat than you think. Bac ha mint, spearmint, hoa hue chives, ngo coriander, aniseedy basil, la lop betel leaves, verbena bong thi la dill. The principal greens include cai tau mustard greens, cai xanh flowering cabbage, rau muong water spinach, cai xoong watercress, cai be trang, Chinese cabbage. Limes or chanh are a fruit you see everywhere in Vietnam and three types are sold: Persian, Thai and kaffir. The kaffir fruit has a bumpy thick skin and

CHAO TOM
SHRIMP PASTE ON SUGAR CANE

This refined dish originated in Hué. If you can't get hold of fresh sugar cane, it's available frozen in Asian supermarkets. There are usually 4 sticks in a packet. I cut them in half crosswise then in half lengthwise, making 16 sticks. Otherwise, use skewers and make balls to thread on them. Pork fat makes the paste tastier and moister. Chao tom are served either on their own with dipping sauce or as a full meal with rice vermicelli, fresh herbs, raw vegetables, rice paper and peanut sauce. You do the wrap up thing, tearing off strips of shrimp paste to put in your roll.

Makes 24

500 g (1 lb) shrimp, shelled and deveined if they are large
60 g (2 oz) diced pork fat or 2 tbsp vegetable oil
6 garlic cloves
2 spring onions or 6 small shallots, chopped
1 tbsp rock sugar
1 tbsp nuoc mam
freshly ground black pepper
2 tbsp roasted rice flour or rice flour
1 tsp baking powder
24 sugar cane sticks, about 8 cm (3 in) long
nuoc cham dipping sauce

1   Make sure the shrimp are as dry as possible by placing them between paper towels – if the paste is too wet, it won't stick to the sugar cane. Place shrimp, pork fat, garlic, spring onions and sugar in a food processor and process till a fine paste. Transfer to a bowl and stir in the nuoc mam, pepper, rice flour and baking powder.
2   Oil your fingers and wrap the shrimp paste around the sugar cane, leaving 2.5 cm (1 in) at the end for holding it.
3   Heat the charcoal grill or oven grill to medium. Spray oil on grill or baking sheet and grill chao tom for 3 minutes on each side.

To serve: Dip sticks in nuoc cham and chew on the remaining sugar cane.

not much juice but the leaves are heavenly, fragrant and very pretty with their double kissing edges. We bought bunches of naughty jasmine flowers – naughty, according to the Vietnamese, because they open up at night, have a seductive perfume and are thus associated with bad girls.

Less seductive and joyful was the roasted dog all piled up on one stand. Madame Mai glossed over this stall but I couldn't take my eyes off the red roasted portions with tails and heads still attached. The teeth were visible as the mouths were pulled back in a cooked grimace. Vietnamese men like to eat dog meat at the end of each lunar month in an orgy of 'inexpressible pleasure'. They believe the meat gives warmth and virility and apparently it tastes of pork with goaty undertones. The preferred breed for eating is 'yellow dog'. Contrary to what I read in guidebooks, the dogs often do not have a swift, humane end. When my director friend Melanie was filming an adventure travel show in Vietnam, her sister witnessed the death of a dog which almost reduced her to hysteria. The dog was strung up by its hind legs and beaten alive before having its throat slit. The adrenaline released as a result of agony and terror is believed to tenderise the meat. A Vietnamese colleague told me of another method of tenderising which is to drown the dog slowly by holding it up by the hind legs and dipping it in and out of water. I believe the Vietcong did this to humans during the war, though not for the same reason. Of course, releasing adrenaline just before death has the opposite effect on meat – it makes it tough. Stress makes the pH level drop and if it is low when the animal is killed, the fluid in the meat will turn to lactic acid, resulting in tough fibres. So if the dogs were kept and slaughtered humanely, the fluid would remain as glycogen and the meat really would be juicy and succulent.

Back at the hotel, we sat around a U-shaped table to watch Madame Mai's cooking demonstration. This lovely, gentle little woman learned to cook and choose the most flavourful and fresh food at her mother's and aunt's knees, then went on to train at the Vietnam Tourism School. She joined the staff at the Metropole kitchen in 1978 and is now second in command to executive chef Didier Corlou. The classes are given entirely in English, which is a little hard to understand, but she does very well, considering she has never lived in an English-speaking country. Unfortunately the written recipes are rather inadequate so you have to watch closely and fill in the missing bits. All the ingredients were neatly lined up at her table and we got to taste everything as it was cooked. One of the most delicious salads you can eat in Vietnam is bap chuoi or banana flower salad. This you can make easily at home if you know someone who grows banana trees in their backyard. You take the huge purple flower, shaped like a long, fat spearhead, remove the outer leaves and slice finely. Place the sliced flower in lemon-infused water for at least half an hour, then rinse it under fresh running water till the water becomes clear. Now you can toss the sliced flower with whatever you fancy. Madame Mai did hers with julienned pork and chicken, mint, bean sprouts and khe or star fruit.

A typical Hanoi speciality is nem or spring rolls made with very fine rice paper. Vietnamese paper is so fine you don't dip it in water, but merely pat it with a damp cloth if you think it necessary. Madame Mai mixed marinated minced pork, du du or papaya, carrots, cu dau or sweet turnip, bean sprouts and vermicelli with beaten egg, rolled it up in the rice paper and fried it. The best part, which I remembered so fondly from my Paris days with Vietnamese friends, was rolling the hot nem up in a crispy lettuce leaf with mint and dipping it in sauce. She grilled chopped chicken wrapped in lemon leaves and stuffed a piece of hollow bamboo with a pork mixture, tied it up and grilled that too. To say the food was delicious would be an understatement; each dish seemed to be more delectable than the last and of course, as each one was cooked, it was passed around for tastings.

Nothing is ever wasted in Vietnamese cuisine. Who would think of sautéing young pumpkin stems and leaves? Madame Mai did, adding lots of garlic and black pepper, which is quite stunning in the north. It is of very high quality, mild, slightly sweet and snappy rather than hot. Using good, fresh pepper in a dish rather than chilli gives a much more complex flavour. The last recipe our little teacher did was one from the modern repertoire of Vietnamese cookery and one you see frequently on restaurant menus – fish steamed with beer and herbs. This dish is obviously French-inspired because there was no beer before they arrived. It's dead simple and very light. Place a whole fish on a bed of herbs and vegetables in a bamboo steamer, cover it with more herbs and vegetables, drown it in beer and steam.

Completely satiated from all our wonderful tastings, we sat back and discussed all we had learnt. The two essentials for Vietnamese cooking are (a) desperate freshness and (b) access to ingredients. If you live in a tree hut in a small town in Texas, forget Vietnamese cooking. Buy a baguette, stuff it with pork paté and crack a beer because, believe it or not, that's also standard fare here. It will never, never taste right if it ain't fresh because it's not only the flavour, it's the mouth feel. Fresh food feels crunchy and alive and good and makes you happy. You can uproot Vietnamese herbs and grow them somewhere else but they won't taste or smell quite the same. None of this is to say it can't be done, simply that it won't taste exactly the same. At this point Madame Mai invited us to have lunch in the Spices Garden restaurant, well known in Hanoi for its dedication to genuine Vietnamese cuisine. It was set up like a buffet of street food, very picturesque with little wooden chairs, bamboo tables, freshly made pho from a stock pot with all the trimmings, tropical fruit, French pastries ... The only things missing were the dirt and the heat.

Several people had told me about Jimmy Pham and KOTO so the next day I set out to find him. Jimmy is an Australian Vietnamese who was in the tourism/travel business. When he visited Hanoi as a tour guide, he was always shocked and concerned by the street kids and wanted to do something to help them. Before long he found himself clothing, feeding and looking after 60 children. Three years later in 1999 he moved to Hanoi and hit on the idea of doing something that would really make a difference – not only caring for the kids but giving them the skills to care for themselves. He set up a restaurant and hospitality training school to teach them marketable skills and give them a sense of pride, self-worth, discipline and responsibility, concepts quite alien to them. KOTO, which stands for know one, teach one, is the name of the school and the restaurant. Jimmy says to his students, 'The greatest accomplishment for the person who has helped you is to see you standing on your own two feet and when you reach your destination, to watch you come back and become a kid brother for someone you met on the street, who reminds you of yourself. Because if you know one, then you should teach one.' KOTO not only has the restaurant and training school with accommodation but a newsletter, website, field trips, sporting activities and working bees to help poor families.

I caught a taxi to the restaurant on Van Mieu Street in the Dong Da district and had a brief interview with him as he ate his lunch, then sucked down a few cigarettes in quick succession. A very sensitive, well-spoken man, probably in his mid-30s, he is pleasant looking, stocky, intense and charming at the same time, and talks in a way that shows he has a million things on his mind. He not only knows how to be Mother Teresa but also how to keep the funds coming in to continue his work (though, let's face it, Mother Teresa was pretty good at that too). As far as I know, Jimmy's isn't a religious calling; he just couldn't stand by, enjoy a cheap holiday and do nothing. The same goes for the Australian volunteers who work at KOTO. The world is actually full of such young people in developing countries who, for personal reasons, are attracted to doing something worthwhile in an exotic location. As Gandhi said, 'Be the change you wish to see in the world.'

The downstairs restaurant is bright and pretty with folding windows onto the street. If you walk past the kitchen full of busy cooks in their whites and go up the stairs, you come to the more comfortable, air-conditioned upstairs restaurant. When you have the privilege of being served by one of these young people, it's hard to believe they haven't come from the best, most loving families; hard to believe some of them were prostitutes, drug addicts, thieves, orphans, living hand-to-mouth in slum hovels. They're so beautiful and engaging and well groomed that they appear to be shining from somewhere within. The service is fantastic and they do it all in English. Jimmy wants them to be able to function in hospitality language and in Vietnam that means English. The food served is both Vietnamese and international.

Most Vietnamese in the service industry are very courteous but I swear you can almost tell a KOTO graduate. I was served tea and cakes at the Metropole one afternoon by a boy who spoke better English and was better dressed than the others, and quietly delightful in his manner. I had a KOTO brochure on the table and when he saw it his eyes lit up.

'You know KOTO, madame?' he exclaimed.

'Yes I do,' I smiled. 'I've just been watching their chef tuition class.'

'Oh madame, I am from KOTO. I stayed there three years and now I am very happy, have a good job and nice place to live. Mr Jimmy very good man.'

In the evening I revised all my 'to do' lists, had a cold shower, spent hours watching the ever-changing street below and the houses opposite, had another shower, wrote and watched TV. My friend Tanah was arriving the next day to travel with me for a few weeks and take photographs. I girded my mental loins to share my travel space with another person. Travel writers tend to be loners mostly by necessity, but then one becomes accustomed to the solitude and pace and it's sometimes hard to slow down for a companion who is really on holiday and therefore in a completely different mode.

2

Ha Long Bay

I knew Tanah's plane had arrived, but hours had gone by and she was nowhere to be seen. Upon arrival at the hotel she was most perplexed to find that I had been there but had gone to Ha Long Bay.

'Are you sure?' she asked the staff, knowing my pedantic reliability in all things.

'Yes, yes, madame. She gone.'

'Red hair with a blonde streak. Peta Mathias. She can't be gone. Has she left a message?'

'No, madame. No message.'

So Tanah sat down on her bed and puzzled and waited for me to come back from Ha Long Bay, a 24-hour round trip. Meanwhile, on the other side of the old quarter, I was tearing my hair out, getting no reply on her mobile and wondering where Tanah was and why she hadn't called me if something had gone wrong. This merry pass went on for a few hours till Tanah suddenly got her brain back and called me on my mobile. What ensued was a farcical set of manoeuvres whereupon we agreed to walk down to the lobby and meet, still talking on the phone. We both got to the lobby and … no one. We were in different hotels of the same name.

A few whiskies and a meal at the upmarket Indochine restaurant smoothed all ruffled feathers. We ate a sort of hotpot called lau sa te, a speciality of the north, where you get to cook your fish, seafood and minced beef in a satay-flavoured stock. The turban-shaped pot comes to the table still sitting on its flame, along with a plate of rice noodles, cabbage and onions. You keep cooking, eating, adding more to the stock, cooking, eating till you are satiated.

'Tanah, how could you think I would take off to Ha Long Bay when when you were arriving from Singapore and we had a definite date?'

'I thought you might have met a mandarin's son who made you an offer you couldn't refuse.'

'This is a Communist country. They don't have mandarins. Why didn't you call me right away?'

'Because they told me you were definitely in the hotel and returning from Ha Long Bay the next day.'

'They lied.'

'Yes, they lied.'

'I wonder why.'

'To keep my business. Do you think the taxi driver was in on it too?'

'Definitely. You gave him the correct address and he took you to his friend's hotel of the same name, knowing you would never know the difference. The rest they played by ear.'

If this sounds like a harsh judgement, we were in Hanoi for over a week, enjoyed the cool interiors of many taxis and were never once taken to the 'wrong' hotel.

As soon as she had settled into the correct hotel, I took Tanah over the road to my market and we sat down to anything that looked scary and unidentifiable. She spotted a stall with all sorts of colourful foods in bowls which turned out to be the ingredients for che ba mau – a sort of dessert drink. We settled in and began to experiment under the helpful tutelage of the 'rainbow drink' princess with soft eyes and shy smile. She took a tall glass, threw in some ice and put whatever you wanted on top from a selection of tiny dried red plums, black, pink and green jelly cubes made from agar-agar, coconut milk, lotus seeds, tapioca pearls, mung beans, azuki beans and sweet sticky rice, topped it up with jasmine water, stuck a long spoon in and voilà. It is the most delicious, cooling drink and gives one strength to approach the tiny fried bird department – the little creatures are eaten whole, bones and all. Small soft crabs are fried live or beaten to a pulp in a big mortar and pestle. There were tables laden with freshly fried nem, chao tom or grilled sugar cane rolled in shrimp paste, ech tam bot ran or battered and fried frogs' legs, sticky rice wrapped in banana leaves, crumbed prawns and freshly fried potato crisps. Everywhere there were large banana leaf-lined baskets of fresh white rice noodles. Tanah, who is a big, voluptuous woman, caused a ripple, or should I say a tidal wave, of giggling throughout the market because of her ample bosom. Several women asked if she could give them some of hers and people kept touching and pinching her plump arms and telling her she was very strong.

And then there was the tofu or dau hu, that mysterious 'poor man's meat' made from soybeans. This, too, was lined up in baskets in all shapes and sizes and three textures – soft for adding to soups and steamed dishes, semi-soft for stir-fries and firm for deep-frying and stuffing. The best in the country, called dau Mo, is made in the village of Mo near Hanoi. All Vietnamese, rich or poor, love tofu but those with a truly discerning palate see the sign dau Mo and jump on it. To make it, the tofu maker first has to buy the best soybeans, which are found in Phu Tho province, 50 kilometres from Hanoi. She picks only the best ones – round, red and of just the right size – then boils them in water for half an hour to clean them. They are carefully ground into a flour which is then put into a large pot of water and boiled again. During the boiling the flame must be very hot and constant or the soybeans will foam and create a film. Next the starch and solid residue is filtered from the water, mixed together and dissolved in boiled yeast water. It is then pressed, and all this has to be done while the tofu is still very hot. It can be cut into many different shapes but the dau Mo is typically cut into a 5 x 2.5-centimetre (2 x 1-inch) rectangle.

The best tofu has a pale, creamy colour, is soft to touch and doesn't really taste of anything. I was advised to buy it in the morning and keep it in water in the fridge. People often say they can't stand tofu because it's so bland but they're missing the point – tofu was not designed to be eaten alone. Its beauty, apart from the high protein and amino acid content and zero cholesterol, is that you can do positively anything with it – grill, bake, steam, fry, poach, throw into a baguette – and turn it into something that looks and tastes like something else. Yes folks, there's a vegetarian restaurant in Hanoi called Com Chay Nang Tam which is famous for creating dishes that are named for and look exactly like meat dishes. If I were a vegetarian, I'd find it beside the point to eat something that tasted and looked like steak but, according to reports, you really can't tell the difference.

One evening we strolled off down to the lake to take in the famous roi nuoc water puppet theatre. Water puppet shows date from the Ly dynasty (1009–1225) and are thought to have been inspired by the annual flooding of the Red River delta, when religious statues floating out of the temples gave villagers the idea for a new entertainment. Historically roi nuoc was performed in thuy dinh, a two-storey village hall where upstairs was used for worship and downstairs for performances. Villagers would gather for shows after harvest or at festival time. There was a head male puppeteer who led the others, none of whom were women. Women were forbidden to join the troupe for fear that, when they married, they would reveal the troupe's secrets to their husband's families.

We lined up and were ushered inside the gaudy theatre to be seated in tiered rows. Everyone sat there fluttering their complimentary fans, waiting with bated breath. Suddenly there was a loud bang and the show was off. The roi nuoc puppet show is hilarious and very noisy with the puppeteers standing waist-deep in water behind a bamboo screen, manipulating the puppets with an arrangement of rods and silk wires on a pulley system. On the left-hand side is the orchestra, dressed in traditional costume, playing flutes, gongs and drums and singing in that high, whiny,

Oriental way, the beauty of which is lost on me. A series of stories is acted out. The four sacred animals – dragon, phoenix, tortoise and unicorn – dance in line and gold and lacquered puppets play out themes of village life and national heroic legends. The most popular character is the chubby peasant compere, Teu, dressed in a red loincloth and black waistcoat. In a loud voice with a huge smile, he tells the villagers off for their bad habits of drunkenness, laziness and wife chasing. The finale is very pretty and clever with fireworks and smoke and clanging gongs. All the children in the audience were absolutely spellbound. At the end the magic of the swimming puppets is revealed – as the male and female puppeteers emerge from behind the screen and bow to wild applause.

On our way home through the crowded streets, we sat down on the low stools at a footpath diner and said, 'We'll have two plates of that, whatever it is, please.' The sign said 'thit bo kho' and it started off with a pile of shredded green papaya and a handful of mint, on top of which was placed sliced dried pork and tongue. This was garnished with chopped peanuts and drenched in a watery sauce. I didn't really see the point of the meat as it had no taste but the overall effect was fragrant and delicious. Tourists stared nervously at us as we smilingly reassured them to give it a go. Back at the hotel a family had set up their electrically powered sugar cane juicing operation across the road. They were there every evening and, in the normal, terrifying Hanoi way, got their electricity from a plug hanging from the apartment above. The man scraped the outer layer off the cane onto the street and the woman fed the rest through the press, the juice dribbling out the other side into a plastic jug. You would be standing there with your salivary glands hurting, waiting for there to be enough sweet juice to fill a glass. She would throw some ice into the glass, top it with juice and pop in a straw. Sometimes she added a squeeze of kumquat, which was heavenly. If you wanted it to go, they put it in a little plastic bag, closed at the top with a straw sticking out.

In the morning, after our pho, we decided to visit Ha Long Bay for real. Before setting off we stopped in at one of the silk shops to have some clothes made, so they would be ready when we got back. Clothes making is a very entertaining and culturally illuminating experience in Vietnam and teaches you a lot about Oriental inscrutability. I would think it also teaches them something about Western capriciousness. For some extraordinary reason, all the guidebooks and travellers' tales make it sound like a snip – you just go in, point and within hours you have a fabulous, perfectly fitted three-piece suit or a copy of Marilyn Monroe's 'Happy Birthday Mr President' dress. Nothing could be further from the truth. It takes hours, days, kilowatts of patience and a powerful fan to stop you from going through the roof. The only thing that would induce you to do it more than once in your lifetime is the knowledge that, although you are only size 12, that is approximately 300 times larger than any Vietnamese woman so you could never simply buy something off the rack, much as you long to. Okay, so if you just say, 'I want three standard shirts', I'm sure it would be easy but if you have one grain of individuality, it's a snake-pit, a bear-trap, a one-way ticket to insanity.

In the shop we went to, all the fabric was folded, one on top of the other on the shelves, rather than on bolts. First you had to have a long discussion about exactly what you wanted, then a long discussion about your choice of fabric, then the girls drew a picture of your fantasy in a book, then they measured you in horrendous detail in the middle of the shop, then they said 'Come back tomorrow at five o'clock and all will be ready.' This is one of the biggest fibs in the universe after 'the cheque's in the mail' and 'but it's you I really love'. Needless to say, we were leaving the next morning to visit Ha Long Bay, and at five o'clock the clothes were not ready, and the ones that were didn't fit properly, but we had to take them because what else could we do? We spent more hours in the shop, sipping tea and waiting.

'I would like this lime green silk for my Chinese top and pants, please.'

'Oh no, madame, you very beautiful but too old. This good colour.'

They show me olive green.

'No thank you.'

'Do you think I would look fat in this colour?' I asked Tanah, who was practically sitting on the fan.

'No. You would look like a fluorescent light bulb but not necessarily fat.'

'I would like piping on the pants, please.'

The dark green comes out.

'Oh no. I want red.'

'*Red?*' Giggle attack.

'Yes. Red as red can be.'

You can't spend time in Hanoi without visiting one of the most beautiful places on earth, Ha Long Bay in Quang Ninh province north of Hanoi. It is one of those mythical places like the French Riviera, Karekare Beach in New Zealand and Krabi in Thailand. It is a UNESCO World Heritage Site and a 'must see', so we jumped into the tourist bus which tried to leave without us, in spite of the fact we were right next to it and had been waiting for 45 minutes. On the highway out of Hanoi, Tanah wondered what Vietnam looked like before concrete, I wondered when the huge water tanks on top of the houses would cause them to cave in and we both wondered why police and throngs of humanity were standing around an old, three-storeyed house. It turned out the construction work going on nearby had loosened the foundations and the house had started to collapse. When we drove back in the next day, sure enough the house was leaning dreadfully and supported by huge pylons. We flew north to Halong past bright green rice paddies dotted with little rose gardens, fish and lily ponds and sometimes a brightly coloured cemetery. Cemeteries in Vietnam are the opposite of the white or grey Western ones. They're like kindergarten playhouses – very ornate in bright pinks, blues, greens and yellows.

Most women you see from the bus window, from farmers to toll guards to bike riders, are hatted and masked, some even gloved, to protect them from the sun. To be pale-skinned in Vietnam is very desirable and the women are never too humble to be concerned about beauty. To be dark shows you work outside and have a rough life. Of course, in the West, it's the opposite. Women lie in the sun to go darker, which is a sign of beauty and shows you have enough leisure time to indulge in such activities. In Vietnam there's no such thing as leisure time unless you're a man. If a woman is wearing a short-sleeved blouse, she wears armpit-length gloves. The hawkers on the beaches look like ragtag gangsters with their conical hats or caps, scarves tied around their faces right up to the eyes, men's shirts done up to the neck, long pants, gloves with the fingers cut out. All this in 35°C (95°F) heat. Since this is what they wear all day every day, I guess their skin will be perfect and they'll look good in their coffins.

Although this was a 'tourist' bus, a quaint name that led us to suppose the driver might have some vestige of concern for our safety, he conducted himself in true Vietnamese kamikaze style. No question of slowing down when he went through a town – just toot louder and longer; bus veering all over the road to double pass; leaving from tea breaks at tourist traps without counting passengers. But this was luxury compared to the 'local' bus – a filthy hell-trap of hilarity with people chewing and spitting, possessions, animals and birds squashed in and leaning out the windows, some people hanging out the back door to keep cool and the top laden with bicycles, furniture, cages of chickens and food. At the opposite end of the scale, if you raised your eyes heavenward, you could see the helicopters of the rich chopping toward the bay. We had bought a ticket on a traditional wooden junk to sail out among the islands, sleep the night on the boat and return the next day. When I look back on it, we were rather trusting – the crew were all very young, we were sitting targets in terms of robbery (especially at night when we were all asleep) and, most dangerous of all, our co-passengers could have been stodgy old bores.

When we reached Halong, a gloved and masked old woman rowed us out to the old-fashioned junk in the bay. There we dumped our bags and popped open the Lanson Black Label Cuvée. Tanah always travels equipped with the necessities of life because you never know when you're going to find yourself in some appalling situation where they expect you to drink water. We put our feet up on the deck, contemplated the cosy décor of bamboo and precious tau wood and waited for the other seven passengers to arrive. The champagne was smooth and creamy, like a fat oyster just before it spawns. An hour later the other inmates arrived, all dressed in cream and beige linen and looking as though they had tripped off the set of a French colonial film. We had obviously misjudged the dress code. Tanah was swathed in a gold and purple sarong, black singlet, gold earrings and an orange silk sarong wrapped around her head and I was dressed down in blue Souliado shirt, red lipstick and Prada shades. We all gaped at each other politely, then moved into the small dining room for lunch.

As the junk sailed out of the harbour, we managed to get through a six-course extravaganza of giant prawns, whole crabs, steamed clams, deep-fried tuna with rice, squid salad and steamed cabbage with fried tofu. The table was beautifully set with white linen and flowers and it turned out that our table mates looked French because they were French. A party of five from Paris consisted of a beautiful, older French Vietnamese woman called Alice, her handsome son Pascal, two lawyer colleagues and an opera singer. This was all very promising, especially as Alice had brought her own home-made nuoc cham sauce which she generously passed around. The other two people were a middle-aged couple from Paris who appeared made for each other — he was a financial adviser and she was a compulsive shopper. She couldn't even be on the high seas without shopping and managed to buy coral, shells (protected, I might add) and table linen without leaving the junk. As quickly as she acquired, her husband gave away. Every time a boatload of miserable people came begging, he gave them all our fruit.

We sat on the deck in cane chairs sipping tea and eating fruit in the salty air, floating past eerie, dark green, limestone islands shaped like fists sticking out of the sea. Halong means 'where the dragon descends into the sea'. The story goes that a dragon lived in the mountains and, as it ran toward the coast, its swishing tail created crevasses and valleys. When it got to the sea it ploughed in, gouging great holes with its powerful tail. These holes filled up with water and only the high bits of land stuck up

— these are the islands of Ha Long Bay. All was calm, all was beautiful on the aquamarine water of the Gulf of Tonkin; in fact it was so calm that the romantic, celebrated purple/red sails of the junk were never raised.

As we drifted past these strange shaped islands, we came across little floating villages of bamboo shacks complete with front porch, hanging washing, fishing boats attached alongside and rickety televisions. The foundations were large empty cans on which the floor was built, the roofs were palm fronds or tin and the walls were made of bamboo strips. The houses were attached to the bay bed by ropes to prevent them floating away. This lifestyle is all right when it's calm but it often rains in Ha Long Bay, and in the summer there are tropical storms that make the water turbulent and dangerous. If a dwelling breaks its moorings, all the young men rush to help the family resecure it with lengths of rubber. People cook, fish, get married, have babies, teach their children to read and write, worship the ancestors and sometimes spend their whole lives on the water in these shacks. How you keep the kids from falling into the 'backyard' is a mystery to me.

Another mysterious and romantic thing about sailing around the islands was the caves and grottoes created by waves and wind. We visited one by climbing up 50 steps then descending into a huge wonderworld of stalactites, waved ceilings and carved pillars, all made by the movement of the sea. The guide was very zealous about communicating to us the financial input of the Chinese in making these caves visitable. The result was *Raiders of the Lost Ark* with Hollywood lighting, an effect only the Chinese would think up; the coloured sets were most bizarre in a natural setting. The humidity was terrific down there so by the time we got back to the boat we were gasping. Our hard work was rewarded by cold facecloths waiting on the deck and a desperately needed plunge. We were very upset by the rubbish in the bay — plastic bags, whole garbage bags, cigarette butts — and watched horrified as passing boat crews threw everything into the water. Fortunately our junk moved to an isolated spot with no people and no rubbish although Tanah saw a floater which she tactfully told me about later. The water was tepid but had a refreshing layer of cold on top from the recent rain. It was very hard to get out and I realised how badly I needed exercise; activity is out of the question in the heat of Hanoi.

Dinner was giant prawns, tomato and cucumber salad with Alice's nuoc cham sauce, whole crab sautéed with ginger, deep-fried calamari balls with fried vermicelli, deep-fried chicken with rice and fried fish. After dinner we ate the bewitching red dragon fruit. When you cut it open, it reveals pure white flesh with tiny black specks, like kiwifruit but white and not as sweet. This was accompanied by tales from Alice in French. Tanah was the only one who didn't speak French but her charm ensured that the others were happy to practise their English on her. Madame Alice Fabre Le Dai is a very cultivated woman with sharp, painted pink toenails, long dark hair in a French roll, stylish Parisian clothes and a fine-featured face with sensuous lips.

'Where are you from?' I asked her in French.

'Je suis de Saigon et j'habite à Paris. This is my first visit to Ha Long Bay – it's like a dream for me. I only started coming back to Vietnam in recent years since the fall of the south in 1975 and this is Pascal's second visit in his whole life. My grandfather was a mandarin and mayor of Long An just outside Saigon. My father never worked in his life – he was a rich playboy gambler. I was a fashion designer and had shops in Saigon before we had most of our property confiscated by the Communists and were forced to leave. You know, the New Zealand ambassador was a client of mine and I remember one day she asked me if I was getting ready to leave Saigon. I said, "No why should I? I'm French and the Americans will protect us." She looked at me with profound pity and it was the first time I understood what might happen to me. The French Saigonais really didn't know or comprehend how bad the situation was. We had no idea what we were in for. I have lived through the Chinese, the Japanese, the French and the Americans and I could tell you stories ….'

She looked off into the distance, gently waving her navy blue fan. I was riveted but didn't want to pry so sipped my iced tea and waited. Et vogue le navire – and the ship sailed on …

'I was very young when the Japanese moved in in 1940 and they didn't stay long – the Viet Minh had got rid of them by 1945. Then there was the French but the sort who came to Vietnam were the dregs, not classy people at all. Then there was the Vietnamese – we did worse things to each other than anyone else had. The Communists killed all the intellectuals, stole everyone's property, burned all the books and raped the women. When I moved to Paris I opened up Vietnamese restaurants and the exiled emperor Bao Dai often came to eat chez moi.'

Alice took some photos from her bag and there she was, gorgeous and dressed in a sparkling ao dai, with the unsmiling Bao Dai and entourage.

'Why is everyone smiling except him? I asked.

'Emperors don't smile,' she replied, 'it's below them.'

'Who is this younger blonde woman with him?'

'That is his last wife Monica whom he married not long before his death in 1998 – she was upgraded from secretary to honorary princess.'

'Not a real princess?'

'Of course not – he wasn't a real emperor any more. Elle se prends toujours pour une princesse celle la,' sniffed Alice. If there were two things that made Alice raise her patrician nose, one was Monica and the other was the Chinese.

'So she got left with all the money.'

'Vous parlez. Il n'avez plus un sou. He was a weak wastrel who gambled all the family money away. His son's not much better. After his father's death he was short of money and sold invaluable family papers, photos and possessions pour rien, for nothing. What the Communists didn't steal in Vietnam, the son got rid of in Paris.'

In Alice's stories the Chinese always came off as sneaky bastards. Her eyes would go cold, there would be a barely concealed sneer and I would glance at Pascal and say, 'Encore ces Chinois.' Also it seemed to me that Ho Chi Minh was generally admired in Vietnam but not his policies or the present Communist party. When I put this to Alice she smartly reminded me he was a ruthless killer and people don't know the half of it. 'It'll all come out about Uncle Ho one day – secret wives, illegitimate children. You watch.' We weren't fussed about the idea of the bus ride back to Hanoi so when Mr Banker and Mrs Spender offered us a lift in their hotel van, we accepted with gratitude.

Back on dry land we went to Quan Com Pho restaurant on Le Van Huu Street where we sank our teeth into moulting crab, rau bi xao sautéed pumpkin stems and leaves, hoa ly xao toi pergularia flowers, which were delicate and delicious, and groper steamed in beer, which was execrable. They obviously didn't know how to do it as the herbs and vegetables, which are supposed to be steamed, were raw. It was inedible and the groper was like foul-tasting rubber underpants. The best part was reading the menu, which served beef steak grilled in spinal cod sauce and red wine Bordelaise, which I guessed was steak with bone marrow and Bordelaise sauce. There was also sautéed chicken intestines and testicles (who would have thought a chicken had testicles?) and grilled goat's burst(?).

The shock of getting some exercise by swimming dementedly around the Ha Long Bay junk 37,000 times exhibited itself in aching bodies, so we took ourselves off to the Dan Chu Hotel in Hanoi for a traditional massage. We were greeted with a chilled glass of jasmine tea and shown to the massage rooms which appeared to be frequented mostly by men. It is well known in Vietnam that these massages can include – gasp – 'extras' of a sexual nature but I'm pretty sure this hotel was straight up in the extras department. As far as I know, no one would even consider giving a woman extras because everyone knows women are in this world to serve, not receive. Tanah gave me great details concerning what young Asian women were taught by their mothers regarding technique and their sexual responsibilities to their husbands.

Once in the air-conditioned massage room which disconcertingly had only partially opaque glass doors, we showered then lay down on the bed. A small towel covered our nether regions and tiny hands got in and did a really hard, deep, all-over massage. They didn't use much cream or oil and the action was more a grabbing than a rubbing movement. It cost US$6 for a full hour and was worth every cent. After finishing each area they did a fantastic vibrating, shimmering movement with their hands all the way down our arms or legs. It felt like an electric current gently passing over the skin. Vietnamese are refined, rather reserved people (when they're not trying to sell you something) and any sort of bodily contact with them, like a massage, is a calming, centring experience, leaving you feeling quite peaceful.

I have to talk about the tourist situation in Hanoi as it's most perplexing. There are lots of them (not the groovy kind as in Bali but the middle management and backpacker kind) but you don't much see them on the streets. I mean, I was out there with the people practically all day and night, save for writing breaks, and I hardly ever saw foreigners eating at the street food stalls. I knew they existed because the hotels were booked to the rafters, but where were they? Did they spend all day in air-conditioned rooms or eating in American style cafés? The fascinated reaction of Hanoi street vendors to Tanah and me slurping down mad delicious things in the gutter, told me we were an anachronism. Without a vestige of doubt, the taste of Hanoi is the taste of the land and the best food is street food. You do have to get over the hygiene and cross-contamination problems and ignore the rubbish all around you, but it's not that bad. In fact, Vietnamese are constantly cleaning up and keeping their little patch in order. They don't have rubbish bins so drop everything on the ground, where it is swept up. By Western standards the entire country would be closed down, but by developing country standards, they do their level best. I ate everything, drank everything, chomped on their ice, used their utensils and only got a tummy upset once in five weeks.

The fact is, Hanoi is just growing too fast and the antique systems can't keep up. As soon as you write about it, it's out of date, they've expanded, the price has gone up, the place has changed hands, tipping is expected. Vietnam is changing by the hour. My up-to-date info said that, in Hanoi, taxi drivers are more or less honest — not true. Eighty per cent will try it on and you have to be very firm. All sellers have two prices, one for Vietnamese and one for foreigners — it's usually about double or sometimes treble for foreigners (very Communist I don't think). People I spoke to who came to Vietnam 10 years ago, say it is unrecognisable.

Astoundingly, the last primitive tribe to be 'socialised' in Vietnam only came out of the jungle completely in 1971. The wild Ruc tribe were discovered in 1959 by border guards on the Laos frontier. They had long tangled hair and were naked save for tree bark tied around their waists. Upon seeing the soldiers they sensibly fled into the jungle and hid in their Ca Rung cave. After five months the soldiers found them, and with the bargaining power of food, persuaded some of them to come out to the 'better life' of regular sedentary farming. They soon regretted it and went back to the caves and the mountains. Not to be put off, the soldiers found the Ruc again and this time offered clothes and medical care as well as food. They came out of the caves once more and tried to settle in a village but made the mistake of choosing a site right on the Ho Chi Minh Trail. When they got bombed to smithereens in the American war they high-tailed it back to the caves. One last time the soldiers talked them out of the jungle into 'civilisation' and the last Ruc people left their shelters in 1971. Their lives have been ruined, of course, because now they are not allowed to smoke or drink and they have to farm instead of throwing the tools away, wear clothes and so on. They drank to ward off the mosquitoes and they smoked for pleasure – by the age of 10 a Ruc child could drink a bowl of wine without getting drunk and was taught to smoke the pipe at the age of two or three. Their narrow valley is still hemmed in by limestone mountains and dense, primeval forests which take three hours to get through, but now, thanks to newly installed satellite dishes, they are addicted to VTV (Vietnamese Television).

For the Vietnamese, family is everything, the centre of the universe, and ancestor worship is very strong. Then comes the village, then the province, then Vietnam. You only have to give them the slightest chance and taste of success and 'following their path' becomes the mantra. They're enormously proud, resilient and famously indomitable people who really want to be successful because they've suffered so much at the hands of the Chinese, the French, Japanese, the Americans, each other, and neighbouring countries like Cambodia. I'd be prepared to bet Communism won't be around in 20 or 30 years either. They want to get to the top, want to make money and spend it and want to have lots of healthy children. Even the poorest people living in abject conditions do their best. The women are good mothers and the houses and food are as good as they can possibly be, given the circumstances.

A great way to find out what's going on in a country, even a Communist one, is by reading local magazines and newspapers. There are several in English and you can usually find the *International Herald Tribune* somewhere, which, even though it is really boring, can always be relied upon to have a fascinating piece of information on exactly the exotic corner of the world you are in. On page three I read that Vietnam had just shut down one of the country's most popular websites for carrying inaccurate and frivolous articles, renewing concerns about media censorship. State media said the site, ttvnonline.com, was shut down because it was improperly licensed and carried information that violated press laws and 'distorted the truth'.

In newspapers, too, I read about a bizarre way of ingesting liquid, practised by the Khang people of the north-west — tu mui or nose drinking. There are only 4000 Khang people left and if strangers try to copy the custom, they feel obliged to kill them, which I think is only reasonable. In the wet season of March when the hot winds blow and the temperature reaches 40°C (104°F), illnesses like cold and flu are common and a medicine of garlic, chilli, citronella (lemon grass), basil and coriander is made. This is pounded to a powder in a copper basin, dissolved in water, then filtered till the liquid is clear. To drink it you put the medicine in an ox horn with a little hole in the tip, tilt your head upward, put the tip of the horn in your nostril, put your tongue at the top of your mouth to close off the bronchial tubes and let the liquid run down your nose into your mouth. If you haven't choked yourself to death, you now begin to sweat the impurities out of your system. This custom is also observed on special occasions such as the lunar new year, harvest celebrations and hunting festivals. The Khang add fermented bamboo liquor (meaning hooch) to the mixture and drink through their noses while eating meat dishes! And they say life is quiet in the jungle …

One very famous Hanoi speciality is the justly exalted bun cha. By chance I was wandering along Hang Manh Street and came across a three-storeyed hothouse of gastronomic ecstasy. Bun cha can be as simple as a few bits of grilled pork thrown on top of some cold noodles and garnished with herbs and sauce on the footpath charcoal grill or it can be the incomparable feast I enjoyed on the first floor of this crowded restaurant. All the windows were closed in the terrible heat and the torrent of vibrating fans was so powerful that you felt as though you were on a yacht in a gale force wind, rounding Cape Horn. I was the only foreigner and didn't have a clue what I was letting myself in for so followed the sign language of the busy, smiling hostess. She pointed to a blue plastic stool at a formica table occupied by office workers. This floor and the one above were absolutely rocking — as soon as a group of people stood up to leave, their places were immediately filled by hordes waiting on the stairs. Everyone was really happy, chatting and slurping, the women sitting ramrod straight, daintily bringing their bowls up to their mouths. A mug of beer, overflowing with ice-cubes, was put in front of me, along with a bowl of tasty broth with daikon radish sliced into it. A huge plate of greens and herbs, a dish of cold white noodles, a bowl of grilled, sliced pork belly which had marinated in caramel sauce, grilled meatballs wrapped in leaves in another sauce and a plate of nem or deep-fried spring rolls completed this feast.

I'm crazy about pork so I was in pig heaven. I watched what others were doing, copied them by popping the plastic bag with the cold face towel, declined to copy those who were crossing themselves (Uncle Ho would be thrilled) and discovered how to eat bun cha. This entails bringing the bowl and the chopsticks up to the mouth, rather than vice versa. Sometimes this involves a lot of action, what with the bowl, the utensils, the beer, the sweat and unwieldy food like long noodles and big nem. You slurp the noodles up and break them off with your teeth at a

NEM RAN HA NOI
DEEP-FRIED SPRING ROLLS

In the north spring rolls are called nem and in the south, cha gio.

Makes 40 rolls

For the filling:
60 g (2 oz) dried cellophane noodles
30 g (1 oz) tree ear mushrooms
500 g (1 lb) minced pork
3 spring onions (white part only), finely chopped
100 g (3$^1/_2$ oz) carrot, peeled and grated
1 egg, beaten
sea salt and freshly ground black pepper

For wrapping and cooking:
500 mls (2 cups) vegetable oil for deep frying
frying thermometer (cheap and essential)
40 small triangular rice papers or 10 large round ones, cut into quarters
1 egg white, beaten

For the garnish:
100 g (3$^1/_2$ oz) bean sprouts
plate of mixed green herbs
plate of lettuce leaves

1   Soak noodles in warm water for 15 minutes, drain and chop up.
2   Soak mushrooms in warm water for 20 minutes, drain and chop finely.
3   Put noodles, mushrooms, pork, spring onions, carrot, egg, salt and pepper in a bowl and mix together with your hands or with chopsticks.
4   Start soaking the rice papers in warm water for a few minutes, 4 at a time. Lay out on a tea towel.
5   Using a pastry brush, coat edges with egg white then place 1 tsp of the filling near the curved side of rice paper. Fold wrapper once over the filling, then the sides and continue rolling to the pointed end. Keep going till all the nem are done.
6   Heat oil in deep pot or wok to 180°C (360°F). Drop nem in to cook 6 at a time for about 3 minutes till they are golden and crisp. Drain on paper towels.

To serve: Take a large lettuce leaf and place some herbs and bean sprouts in the middle. Put a spring roll on top and roll it all up in the lettuce leaf. Dip in nuoc cham and go to heaven.

Nuoc Cham
Dipping Sauce

Makes about 2 cups
2 cloves of garlic
2 small fresh red chillies, sliced, seeds removed
4 tbsp sugar
3 limes producing about $1/2$ cup lime juice
3 tbsp water
$1/3$ cup nuoc mam

In a mortar and pestle, pound garlic, chilli and sugar into a paste.
Squeeze lime juice and put aside. Remove the lime pulp from the skin
with a small knife and pound it into the paste. Add lime juice, water and
nuoc mam and stir well. Will keep for 2 weeks refrigerated.

Alternative lazy method:
Beat together the sugar, lime juice, water and fish sauce till sugar has
dissolved. Add chopped garlic and chilli.

given point, and if the nem is big, you delicately nibble at it over the bowl
which is now close to your face. You just keep piling things into your
bowl – noodles, then pork, then meatballs, then greens, then nuoc cham,
then daikon, then start over again. The pork was smoky, sweet, sour, hot
and salty all at the same time and the finely minced pork meatballs had
been seared on the charcoal grill so that they were aromatic on the outside
and unbearably tender and juicy on the inside.

You end up drinking gallons of beer to replace the sweat. Most beer in
Vietnam is brewed locally because the taxes on imported beers are so
outrageous that no one can afford them. If you make the mistake of
ordering an imported beer in a cheap restaurant, it will probably cost more
than the entire meal. In colonial times the French made very good beer,
but production ceased when almost all French companies were given their
marching orders in 1975. In the 1990s the French company BGI was
allowed back in on the tide of economic and social liberalisation or doi

moi and began producing delicious Tiger beer, a resurrection of the old label. Tiger beer is second in consumption only to the 333 brand, pronounced 'ba-ba-ba'. The working Vietnamese themselves drink a sort of fresh beer like draught called bia hoi, introduced to them, bizarrely, by the Czechs. When I say fresh I mean fresh. Like Vietnamese baguettes, which are meant to be eaten within the hour, bia hoi is made without preservatives to be consumed that day. It costs about 15 cents (US) a glass and, as with most beer in Vietnam, they fill it with huge chunks of ice before you can stop them. Bia hoi is very light and very burpy so best not drunk on an empty stomach. It is usually served in beer 'garages' and only to men who, in spite of its lightness, get incredibly drunk on it. The best thing about these garages apparently is the good snack food that is always served with fresh beer.

On the open ground floor of this restaurant, which extended right out to the street, the kitchen was in full swing with a dishwashing corner, a greens washing and a prep area. Industrious, smiling staff were locking that pork into the little grill and barbecueing it, making the delicate, moist meatballs and putting those, too, in the grill, deep-frying nem. And it was all done by hand and all in small batches, which was why it all tasted as if it was made for you and you only — because it was. Quail were wandering around perilously close to the cooking pot. Didn't they know these people would have them in that pot in a matter of minutes? The real way to cook bun cha is over coals between two bamboo sticks which are thrown away at the end of the day. Traditionally, therefore, it's a meal that can only be cooked outside because of all the smoke it produces.

Just around the corner is dim, slummy Dong Xuan Ngo alley where you get the 'real thing' plus those great che or rainbow drinks. Drenched in sweat, I gladly plonked myself down at a stall and started pointing to shaved ice, coconut milk, dried banana, dried apples and lychees. One girl, who spoke a little English, said all the ladies wanted to know how old I was. When I told them they exclaimed, 'Oh no madame, not possible, you too young. This drink very good for bed, you husband happy tonight.' So the girls *do* have aphrodisiacs. Further down the shady alley I saw a woman

BANH GOI
NOODLE PILLOWS

400 g or 2 cups cooked egg noodles
vegetable oil for frying

Divide the noodles into equal amounts of 4 or 6 and fry in little bundles
or pillows till golden on the bottom. Carefully turn over and brown the
other side, about 2 minutes. I place the noodles in little pastry rings to
ensure they stay round but the Vietnamese make perfect circles by
nature. Place sautéed vegetables or whatever you wish on top and serve
with nuoc cham.

frying cooked egg noodles in little bundles. When they were golden on
both sides, she plopped stir-fried vegetables on top and served them with
two different sauces; these she called noodle pillows. Very taken by such
a charming name, I resolved to try this method when I got home.

Tanah and I really liked Hanoi and could easily have stayed longer but I
knew that, if I was going to write this book, I had to keep moving. There
were things we didn't do, such as admiring the French colonial
architecture with its old ochre buildings, because we were much more
interested in our life in the old quarter. We liked the lakes and parks and
strolling after dark, watching people shadow boxing under the trees and
licking ice creams. We didn't like the ruthlessness and brutality of the
police towards poor people trying to make a living. Peasant women selling
illegally on the street would be kicked and screamed at to get out of the
way. Hanoi police were so notorious for harassing foreigners that outside
investors just went straight to Saigon, but they have been forced to pull
their heads in recently as economic reform has swept the city. This
viciousness is a remnant of the days when Ho Chi Minh made the area a
police state, rampant with denunciations, detentions, black listings and
atrocious human rights violations.

Tanah's room at Classic Street hotel was across the courtyard from mine so we could have conversations without using the phone. We packed our bags, calling to each other not to forget this and that, folded down the laptops, packed the digital camera, retrieved the gin and red wine from the fridges, grabbed the bunches of hairy red rambutans, said fond goodbyes to the staff whom we now adored and jumped into a taxi for the airport. I had decided to head for the centre of Vietnam and our first stop would be the old imperial city of Hué. Our taxi was driven by a gentleman who had no acquaintance whatsoever with a clutch and drove in fourth gear the whole way. Tanah was convinced he was smacked out on opium so we sort of glided to our destination, passing hondas and bicycles with at least a dozen unfortunate geese hanging upside-down by their feet, struggling to keep their beaks from scraping the ground. When Tanah remarked that there were no dogs or cats on the streets, the driver told us people do have cats as pets but they hide them at home because the Chinese (encore ces Chinois) eat them. And we already know what happens to the dogs, n'est-ce pas?

3

Hué

In my continuing quest for the definitive pho, Tanah and I caught the smelliest taxi in the history of the world – surely it had a fish sauce factory in the boot – from the airport in Hué. The first hotel we stopped at had been recommended by a friend. It was entirely unsuitable and didn't pass any of the non-negotiable qualities we required, which included charm, location and nuttiness of some description. Next we drove over the river to a hotel the Classic people in Hanoi had recommended. The Thanh Noi was just the ticket, set back from the street in a quiet village on the north side of the Perfume River, a one-storey place with utterly over-the-top faux imperial decor. The best rooms, which of course were already gone, looked out onto the tree-shaded compound, a short walk from 'the intelligent swimming pool'. After swapping rooms a few times, we finally settled on two that were graced with kitsch wall lamps, brown and gold furniture, pale sherbert-green, shiny, polyester curtains and what I call 'multiple insurance' showers. You get general cover and don't need to move – the shower sprays the entire bathroom because there's no shower unit, and you spend the rest of the night walking water all over your room. This is particularly exciting when trying to plug your laptop into the faulty wiring. I got lots of electrical shocks in Vietnam and my skin has never been better.

We had developed our own Indochine gin and tonic with a squeeze of the delicious kumquats and a wave of spicy Vietnamese mint. Into this we threw an ice-cube the size of Texas, put our swollen feet up the wall vertically and sipped. Sometimes drinking in this position meant the liquid ran down the neck rather than the oesophagus. This wasn't as disagreeable as it sounds; in fact, in desperation one morning, I cleaned my teeth in gin and tonic. This cocktail hour bridged the gap between afternoon heat exhaustion and evening strolls to exotic village locations such as the enchanting Tinh Gia Vien restaurant run by master chef Madame Ha. On our walk we discovered that we, our hotel and almost everywhere we wanted to eat were actually within the moated Kinh Thanh or citadel (ancient royal city). Just down the road, the heart of the citadel – the Forbidden Purple City – sat mysteriously in the tepid darkness, speaking to us of another centuries-old life, now lost. The citadel is a calm, relaxed place, like a beautiful, sleepy village; in fact the original name for Hué Hoa means harmony or transformation. Eventually, after wandering past open houses with folks watching television, garden bars with fairy lights and chatty people helping us on our way, we came to our destination.

Tinh Gia Vien restaurant is in a private mansion and entering the property is akin to infiltrating an enchanted land. The gardens are gorgeous, resplendent with tropical flowers, fountains, spectacular bonsais and lush trees, all illuminated with twinkling lanterns and candles and little lights. Ornate red and gold tables are set on the large balconies and the waitresses are dressed in traditional Hué costumes with halo-like headdresses. All is peace and tranquillity: all that can be heard is the rasping of cicadas and the chattering of contented diners. It says on her card that Madame Ton Nu Ha is descended from the Nguyen emperors and is therefore a specialist in nutrition, gastronomy, culinary art and bonsai creation. If you don't believe her, go and look at the website or one of the many albums full of photos of her culinary creations. Hué is renowned for its intricate and delicious imperial haute cuisine and most of those cooking it are women who can trace their lineage back to the royal household. Personally I can't get worked up over carrot flowers and papaya dragons but apparently the emperors in the forbidden palace were mad for them. A succession (10 courses in all) of ever more extravagant peacocks, dragons, fish, chickens and porcupines composed of pâté, minuscule spring rolls, mushrooms, squid, vegetables and fruit, marched across our table. In all honesty, the food was very ornate and visually pleasurable but not massively flavourful and with a whiff of the production line. For me the most tasty dish was the chicken soup loaded with lotus seeds (which I've come to love) and fresh Vietnamese black pepper.

Madame Ha visited each table personally and spoke warmly with everyone. Incredibly charming, like most Vietnamese, she had a vivacious personality and limitless energy. She invited us into the large kitchens out the back, half of which were outdoors. In the garden kitchen huge cauldrons were boiling and bubbling, toiling and troubling over open fires. Inside, what seemed like dozens of girls were quietly cooking, chopping, frying, mixing and arranging this delicate food. No one appeared rushed, just doing their little job in the heat with no air-conditioning or ventilation save the doorway. Someone was soaking a dried, very aromatic version of nuoc mam called mam tom, a speciality of Hué, made with shrimp instead of fish. Such is its strength, the American soldiers used to call it Vietcong tear gas.

In principle imperial Hué cuisine, presented in small amounts on many plates, is more refined than anywhere else in Vietnam. The cooking techniques are sophisticated, the service is rather formal and, of course, appearance is everything. The food is seasonal, unlike dishes in the rest of Vietnam, and the cooks use unusual locally grown vegetables such as potatoes, tomatoes, asparagus, artichokes, green bananas, green corn and cauliflower. In spring they eat aubergines, calabash, pumpkins, seafood and birds, especially duck; in summer, pickles, light vegetables, fish and tropical fruit like mangosteen and jack fruit; in autumn they dive into all sorts of beans, prawns and fruits such as pomelo, tangerine and persimmon, and in winter out come the preserved vegetables, river fish, game birds, green peas and bitter melon. Hué pigs are the tenderest and sweetest in Vietnam because they're fed on banana tree greens and rice. All this is turned into complex delicacies, but where did all these ideas come from?

Once upon a time in the 19th century there was an emperor of the Nguyen dynasty called Tu Duc who was a philosopher, poet and intellectual. He wished to eat only ecstasy and beauty, never to consume the same meal twice in a year and to be served in a ritualistic, artistic way by desperately gorgeous maidens. As the women of Hué are famous for their beauty, this was not difficult to achieve. His meals consisted of 50 tiny dishes at every sitting, cooked by 50 cooks and served by 50 servants, so there are literally thousands of recipes in the imperial repertoire. The centre of Vietnam lacks the luscious agricultural variety of the south, so Tu Duc's chefs had to be very inventive by deconstructing and refining ordinary dishes, disguising ingredients as other things and inventing previously unheard of combinations. The emperor also raised tea drinking to sublime artistic heights, loaded with aesthetic content and intellectual meaning. He insisted his tea be made with dew collected from leaves overnight, which I don't find unreasonable. I mean, if you've got the staff ...

It's not only the imperial cooks of Hué who are good; from homes to cheap restaurants to street stalls, the food is great. To eat at Lac Thien restaurant on the north side of the river, you have to know where you're going and be determined to get there, because there's Lac Tanh next door and Lac Thuan around the corner. They all have deaf staff and they all appear to be the same, but don't be tricked by the Vietnamese talent for copying. Lac Thien is the destination you want. It's small, has an upstairs, is pretty messy and nothing would tell you there's anything special about it until you eat the meal they are most famous for – banh khoai or happy crepes. They're also famous for their wonderful hospitality. The father, Me Le, is deaf and dumb but none of his seven daughters is. They all work there and they all look very alike. His last child is a little boy who is, of course, the centre of the universe. He greets you as if you're a long-lost friend, with open arms, ear-to-ear smiles and effusive (silent) welcome gestures. One of the daughters explained the pièce de résistance to me while grandma and a younger sister cooked them. Grandma Ho Thi Tra had long grey hair in a bun, black betel-stained teeth and a fat, hand-rolled cigarette hanging out of her mouth. She smiled all the time.

The kitchen has to be seen to be believed. It's very typical of Vietnamese restaurants — a long, ill-lit galley with blackened walls, blackened woks, clay pots and pans, a shrine to the kitchen god, big bowls for dish washing, black gas burners, mesh implements and bowls for washing, cooking, scooping, blanching. Vietnamese kitchens always boast an array of sharp, flat knives with wooden handles, big choppers, ingenious vegetable peelers and shredders, skewers, long chopsticks for stirring and scooping, spoons, a mortar and pestle and clay pots. No dishwasher, no fridge, no pre-packaged food — everything on the benches is fresh and replenished from the market twice daily. It takes much longer to prepare finely chopped Vietnamese food than to cook it.

The happy crepe cooking happened outside at the front of the shop on charcoal burners. A lot of food in Vietnam is cooked over charcoal, which gives it heavenly smoky flavours, impossible to replicate with any other system of cooking. The happy crepe is a cross between a crepe and an omelette, is small and combines both seafood and meat, common in Hué cuisine. They use little 10-centimetre frying-pans with long handles. They heat a bit of peanut oil, into which goes the crepe mixture and on top of that prawns, pork paste, bean sprouts, onion and mushroom. The pan is covered for a few minutes then some egg mixture is poured in. After being covered again for a few minutes, the crepe is folded in half, and more oil is added. The crepe is done when it is very crispy. The excess oil is poured off and the crepe is slid onto a plate and placed in front of your grateful eyes. It is accompanied by a big plate of greens and herbs, garlic, chilli, peanut sauce, nuoc cham and sliced star fruit and green banana. You rip off pieces of the crepe and make a package of it with the accompaniments in a lettuce leaf. This meal satisfies on many levels — you get to play with your food, it sounds good when you crunch into it, it has many different textures and it tastes fabulous, especially with litres of ice-diluted beer.

BANH KHOAI
HAPPY CREPES

Serves 6

For the crepes:
120 g (1 cup) rice flour
60 g ($^1/_2$ cup) cornflour (cornstarch)
30 g ($^1/_4$ cup) white wheat flour
560 mls/18 fl oz (2$^1/_2$ cups) water
3 spring onions, green and white parts finely sliced separately
250 g (8 oz) minced pork
2 tbsp nuoc mam
2 cloves of garlic, minced
freshly ground black pepper
250 g (8 oz) shelled prawns or shrimp
250 g (8 oz) bean sprouts
1 small onion, sliced
half a dozen button mushrooms, sliced
3 eggs, beaten
peanut or vegetable oil
10 cm (4 in) frying-pan, preferably with long handle

For the garnish:
big plate of salad greens and herbs like coriander, mint, verbena, basil and parsley

saucer of peeled garlic	saucer of chopped chilli
saucer of sliced starfruit	saucer of sliced green banana
bowl of peanut sauce	bowl of nuoc cham

1   Mix together the flours and water to make a smooth batter. Stir in spring onion greens.
2   Mix together the pork, 1 tbsp of nuoc mam, half the garlic and spring onion whites and a few good twists of black pepper.
3   Mix together the shrimps, 1 tbsp nuoc mam, the rest of the garlic and spring onion whites and some pepper.

4   Heat a tbsp of oil in the frying-pan to hot, then pour in 3 tbsp of
    batter and cook for a minute. On top of this dot $1\frac{1}{2}$ tbsp of pork
    mixture, some prawn mixture, some sprouts and a few slices of onion
    and mushroom. Cover and cook another few minutes.
5   Uncover, pour in 3 tbsp of the beaten egg, cover and cook for another
    few minutes.
6   Uncover, fold the crepe in half, adding more oil if needed. Cover and
    continue cooking for another few minutes, turning occasionally, till it
    is very crispy.

To serve:
Rip pieces of crepe off and place them in a lettuce leaf along with some
herbs and any of the other garnishes you like. Wrap up, dip in sauce and
crunch away. Drink lots of ice-diluted beer.

The family are always hovering around solicitously, touching your arm
and explaining how things are done.

During lunch I broached with Tanah the topic of my roots. My hair
needed seeing to; it had been a month since I had darkened the doors of
a salon and I felt if I could survive the dressmaker, I could survive the
hairdresser. Tanah looked nervous but was keeping an open mind in the
interests of research. We strolled across to the new town on our daring
mission and discovered that the hairdressing joints in the big hotels
required appointments. I, however, was into instant gratification with all
its risks, so after traipsing to three recommended places, we ended up at a
salon down by the river. What followed was a truly terrifying cultural
experience. Never mind the risk of snakes, typhoid and malaria – get your
hair coloured at a local, tinpot salon. Obviously very minimal English was
spoken so I innocently pointed to my hair and showed them the L'Oreal
recipe my hairdresser at home had carefully written in my diary.

'Okay, okay, madame. We no have L'Oreal but no problem. Sit down,
sit down.'

I sat down and a boy jumped on a bike and raced off down the street.

'You want hand massage? You frien want hand massage?'

'No. No thank you.'

I then received a hand massage.

'You want face massage, madame?'

'No thank you. I want my hair done.'

Ten-second pause.

'Okay, I'll have a face massage.'

Every muscle in my face was rapidly and brusquely rearranged. In the middle of it, the aforementioned boy arrived back from bike dash and excitedly presented me with some products I had never heard of.

'Thank you very much but this is not L'Oreal.'

'No L'Oreal, madame. Only this.'

Tanah was looking at me with saucer eyes. 'Peta, I can't believe you're going to do this.'

'I know I might end up with black and orange hair at best, but this is a cultural experience, Tanah. It's me and the people.'

'Christ.'

'Why don't you have your hair done too?'

'Are you kidding? I'm going for a walk.'

All kinds of thoughts were running through my mind. My hair is one of the trademarks of my television food show, so can my identity take ruined hair? Do I care? What does it have to do with world peace? Bush is talking about blowing the daylights out of Iraq and I'm worried about the risk of a bad hair day. I asked the staff (really just boys and girls) for their colour charts. I was given one small chart with a dozen colours on it and that was it; that was the choice. So between us, and anyone else who walked by, I decided on my colour mixture. Bizarrely, they insisted on washing and drying my hair first. Then a boy and girl worked on me, one either side, with four others giving advice. The boy on the left did a hatchet job and the girl on the right carefully isolated every single strand of the blonde streak and tied it up in a little knot. In a complete absence of method, they painted on a bright orange paste, reeking of ammonia, ignoring the roots till I pointed them out. They then walked away, very happy with their work.

'What about the blonde bit?'

'Later, madame.'

'No. Now please.' I had visions of still being there the next day.

Someone found a plastic supermarket bag, tied it around my scalp, cut a hole in the top and pulled the blonde bit through.

Tanah walked in as they were applying powder blue paste and screamed. 'Oh my God. Where's my camera … where's my camera … tell them to wait till I focus!'

One of the boys picked up the brush with leftover blue paste on it and combed it into his black hair. A light went on in my traumatised brain and I realised the dye would be for Asian hair, which is completely different from European hair. By then I was convinced the blue would make my hair fall out and the orange would be purple so I asked them to wash it out, which they did with conditioner, not shampoo. At this very moment the electricity cut out, which happens often in the monsoon rain, so no hairdryer. I haggled over the price and finally agreed on US$20, which was far too much. This whole episode took two and a half hours. If I had stayed for styling, they would have had to bring in my dinner and a bed to which I would also have had to be tied.

Since aggression and hunger are closely related in the brain, rather than screaming I felt an overwhelming need to eat. Tanah suggested we go back to Lac Thien, where she knew nothing could go wrong, so we ran out into the rain, hailed a taxi, jumped out at the restaurant and fell into the family's open arms. I looked down at my white linen top and noticed it was stained with red dye from my dripping hair. The electricity was still down but locals hardly notice this sort of thing any more – the women were in the kitchen chopping and cooking as if it didn't make the slightest difference. It was business as usual in the restaurant and we sat down gratefully, wiping away a combination of rain and sweat. Looking around, I saw two people eating a beautiful meal and asked if they could point to it on the menu.

The well-coiffed, smooth-skinned man smiled and said in French, 'Ce n'est pas sur la carte. You have the tourist menu. I'm Vietnamese so I just ask for what I want and they make it.'

'I want exactly what you've got.'

'Okay, I'll order it for you.'

What turned up was canh chua ca, a light, fragrant, sweet and sour broth floating with tomatoes, shaved bamboo, greens, pineapple, onion, leeks, fresh black pepper and fish. It was heavenly. This colourful, unusual combination of ingredients is typical of Hué cuisine, as is the sour taste that comes from tamarind (a Thai influence). Then a plate of trung ran voi thit bam or northern omelette arrived, a flat omelette full of tasty things, along with rau muong xao thit bo — water spinach with beef and a bowl of rice of course. Every so often grandma would feed me titbits from the bowl of fish, turnip chips and shrimps she was eating as she wandered about. The restaurant seemed to be full of love and happiness and if we hadn't had so much other food to try, we probably would have eaten every meal there. We finished off with the best and smallest creme caramels we had yet eaten. The Vietnamese are so in love with creme caramel, they've forgotten they didn't invent it. The French gave it to them and they often improve on it by making it with half cream and half coconut cream.

We got to talking about imperial cuisine with our gastronomic guide at the other table. His name was Thierry and he gave us the name of another imperial restaurant in a private mansion called Y Thao. Then Dad came over and did his bottle-opening trick for us. He has invented a bottle opener made out of a stick of thin wood with a nut and bolt screwed into it. You place it over the top of the bottle, give it a good whack with the side of your hand and bang! the lid flies off. Every time he did his trick, everyone clapped and marvelled at how clever and ingenious it was. He gave us an opener each, signed and dated.

Back at the hotel, I washed the equivalent of the Red River down the shower. My hair was now mahogany with an iridescent white streak, not unlike the lightning outside, I frightened old women and small children and my career as a television presenter was over.

It was just after the cyclo carrying the cow passed us, that we had our very own cyclo accident. I had been riding on cyclos and hondas since our arrival in Vietnam but Tanah had refused to, saying they were too dangerous. Once I had finally convinced her that nothing would happen to us, we got into two cyclos to go to the market and a honda drove straight into Tanah. What can you say? The driver had a cut leg, Tanah a bruised shoulder, the honda passenger was banged about a bit and the driver, of course, was unhurt. After everyone had limped around yelling at each other for a while, we decided that perhaps we would walk to the market after all. Nobody was concerned about the wounded; the only concerns were for the vehicles. At this a huge fight ensued and we backed off into the greenery, eventually ending up at the Dong Ba market to try out the bun bo. It was a rather slutty market with a lot of very poor people all desperate to sell us something. We sat down in the muck, surrounded by begging people, and ate bowls of broth, noodles, meat, tongue, greens, bamboo shoots, chilli and banana flowers. Then we bought some rainbow drinks for everyone and handed them around. Big smiles everywhere. This was the first time in Hué we had eaten anything that resembled pho. In Hué it had a different name, bun bo, and different ingredients from its northern counterpart. Hué is famous for vermicelli soups. Each province seems to have its own variation of pho. I was told the best phos are made at home. For example, there's a glass noodle and chicken soup called mien ga and an egg noodle and roast duck soup called mi vit. A more unusual version of pho is hu tieu do bien, made with a pork and dried squid stock and served with shrimp and flat noodles.

We were so lucky to be staying on the left side of the Perfume River. All the advice had said to stay on the right but on this peaceful side we found our favourite sugar cane and kumquat pressing lady and a place making banh bao — rice flour buns stuffed with pork, quail eggs, herbs and vegetables. These were kept warm in steamers — you pulled them open with your fingers and dived in. Then there was the candle-lit Han Thuyen Street on the edge of a square near our hotel, which woke up only at night. On one side of the square there were bars full of drunken men but on the other side stalls were set up on the street, all selling exactly the same thing in the hot, twinkling, firefly night. This was the hangout for everybody in town – teens screeching in on their bikes, girls in raincoats perched on the back, families, visitors – and it was pumping under the cool, leafy trees. The meal everyone was so keen to get down their gullets was a variation of pho made from a mildly spicy broth, fat, slightly sour noodles, sliced meat and quail eggs garnished with limes and chilli sauce. We consumed side orders of spicy sausage wrapped in banana leaves, tied together in fours, then steamed. It was very good with beer. We got charged twice as much as the Vietnamese patrons, which we accepted because we couldn't be bothered arguing yet again over yet another price, but when the heavens opened and the raincoat seller mysteriously appeared and tried to charge us 5000 dong for 2000 dong coats, we stood our ground. We got wet but we stood our ground. All this double charging is done with the most charming smiles and friendly, open faces.

Back at the hotel the storm really hit. The generators thumped away in the relentless rain, doors banged all night and I lay on my bed listening to these noises of the tropics. Next morning the Perfume River was right up, the rice paddies were flooded but not destroyed and the rice paddy frogs had come out. Vietnamese love eating these little critters and wander around the paddies at night with lights on their heads, looking for them. As soon as we got a break in the rain, we went to visit the Forbidden Purple City – 15,000 dong (US$1) for Vietnamese, 50,000 dong (US$3) for foreigners – and I bought a photocopied booklet on the ladies and empresses of the Nguyen household. The translation of this book was so outrageous they should have been embarrassed to sell it, but it did give me a few insights into the cloistered lives of these women. In fact, not a lot is known about them, because once they were inside the purple tetragonal walls, no one ever saw them again and their lives were considered only their husband's business (and they all had the same husband). Only eunuch males were allowed to have anything to do with the royal concubines.

Girls were selected for concubinage by scouts of the king and verily summonsed. They could be chosen for their virtuousness, talent or beauty, or because they were related to powerful mandarins, though they came from all ranks of society. One monarch who got restless would disguise himself as a student to walk around Hué. One day he fell in love with the lovely oars girl on his boat, offered to row for her, then asked her if she'd fancy a change of lodgings. The next thing she knew, she was an aristocrat. It was a great honour for a family to give their daughter to the royal court but very boring for the girl because you were taken away from your family at a young age – 15 on average – and you might never get near the emperor in your whole life anyway. You were there as a status symbol and the emperor wasn't really aware of you unless you were, for some reason, chosen for his bed one night.

So you had to do something to entertain yourself and prevent insanity and melancholia. The other concubines were no fun because the whole outfit was riddled with jealousies, one-upmanship and sexual frustration. Imagine if you were a beautiful young woman and you had never known romance, sex and childbirth – the norms of every woman's life. The emperor didn't know you existed but the other nobles in the court did, and you spent your waking hours plotting and scheming and making trouble and setting up secret but desperately dangerous love trysts with other nobles within the forbidden city. These trysts, which happened at night, have been described as like nocturnal bats flying for prey. If you were caught, you got the chop and your family suffered for the rest of their lives. According to a courtier who hung out on the back steps of the palace after a court gathering, 'I see wrathful scenes and conflicts from slanderous fights. At my sight they rush over in untidy clothes, crying out with angry and painful face gestures. My arrangement will be required from the females in clamours.' If you didn't understand that, try reading a book full of it.

Women not only had few rights in this ancient Confucian society, they were also verbally abused, humiliated and ridiculed by the males who had power over them. It was considered more difficult to control these ladies than to rule the whole nation or win a battle. Needless to say, what with the tediousness of life and the ban on openly expressing emotion, the women often suffered from depression. Not only could you not say the names of the royal family, you couldn't even express certain things verbally and your behaviour and gestures were controlled. You couldn't say a sick monarch was 'in pain', you had to say 'aching'; a 'walk' was called 'an imperial pacing'; it was forbidden to use such negative words as blindness, lameness, bleeding, leprosy or killing. It took about six months for the courtiers to learn this language and they were fined if they slipped.

When the concubines became physically ill, woe betide them, because no physician was allowed to see or touch them. The most they could do was take the pulse through a silk wrapping before making a diagnosis without looking at the patient's face or speaking to her. Most of the women died young, never having left the four walls of the palace compound. The only way they could leave was if there was a natural disaster like a flood or a fire or during political unrest. On the occasion of a three-year drought, an emperor reasoned that 'the court maids are so many that the negative and feminine airs halt the natural courses. A reduction of about a hundred maids can solve the natural disaster' so they were sent home to their families to be commoners again. If the court had to evacuate owing to political unrest or a battle, a lot of the women never went back and chose to go home. The best thing that could happen to you was to have a child because it gave you something to do and someone to love. According to my source, the other way to die would be by accompanying your monarch to the mausoleum when he died, although the concubines and wives were not buried alive with him as in other cultures.

As in any other royal court, the female courtiers were ranked in order of importance. After the queen were the Phi or first wives, then the Tu or marquises, then the Cua Tan or countesses, then the Chieu or viscountesses, then the Sung or baronesses. In literature, the queens and first wives are always described as faithful, motherly, brave, humane, decent, tender, learned and fascinating; they submitted to their narrow, tiresome lives with grace. But there was, of course, naughtiness. In 1883, the 22-year-old widowed princess Dong Xuan had an incestuous affair with her half-brother. When this was discovered by the court, he was exiled and mysteriously liquidated and she was demoted to commoner, though subsequently reinstated by the next emperor, under the condition she bring up her children properly in the court and remain penitent for the rest of her life.

The three most important women in the court were the monarch's mother, his maternal grandmother and his wife, in that order. The grandmother (Grand Maternal Empress) had her own palace outside the main walls and enjoyed a staff of 60 ladies, ladies-in-waiting, maidservants, entertainers and eunuchs. The mother (Maternal Empress) had an even grander palace outside the gates comprising pools with floating pavilions, fountains, theatres and huge kitchens. The queen or Treasured Lady's palace was within the forbidden city, just behind the king's, and the top two concubines lived in a residence behind that. To the west and the east of the king's palace, lay the accommodation of the lesser concubines, servants and eunuchs. Ageing maids or ones who were losing their looks served as cleaners and young, pretty ones brushed hair or lay around the queen's bed at night to protect her. They were paid in money and in rice. Way out in the backblocks somewhere were the slaves, who spent their whole lives kneeling and were, of course, paid nothing. If they had been any lower in life they would have been fertilising the soil.

The most powerful of all these women was the queen mother, who could actually influence the king; he had to bow to her in matters of etiquette and morality. If she disapproved of the offspring of a concubine, that child never reached any position of authority. Tu Duc's mother changed all the plays and operas that were performed in the court, by eradicating all murders, even if they were based on fact. As for the empress, although she was waited on hand and foot and wore silk satin yellow robes, her life was not easy. She had many tedious responsibilities, which meant going to bed late and getting up early to fit them all in; she had to watch her back constantly for criticism and treachery from the concubines; if she made one mistake, the reaction from the emperor was pathological. Because Tu Duc's wife brought his dinner late one evening when he was ill, she lost her position of leadership. This was a woman who was a princess in her own right and had been in service (that's what they called marriage) to the king for 32 years.

To my mind the most interesting characters in the court had to be the eunuchs, another group we know very little about. Known as 'emasculatees' or 'effeminatees', they were either born without properly developed sexual organs or castrated themselves to get the job. This I find hard to believe – I would think their families probably forced this on them. Their coat of arms sported a phoenix and they wore green gowns woven with red flowers and flat, oval hats. In the writings on the court, any bad or 'evilous' eunuchs were described as Chinese and good ones as Vietnamese. One evilous eunuch killed his child (how did he get a child?), cooked it and served it up to the king to curry favour, no pun intended. Sometimes they were so powerful and machiavellian as to topple a kingdom. Now here's an interesting fact that I hadn't thought of: obviously the 'effiminatees' were homosexuals who got up to all sorts of exploits with each other, but some of the high-ranking male courtiers were also gay and proud of it, so the evenings must have been very busy. As time went by fewer and fewer eunuchs came into royal service because they missed not having their own children to worship at their altars after they died. Ancestor worship is very important in Vietnamese culture and because eunuchs' lives were pitiable and rather sad they made a financial arrangement with the emperor to have their own very beautiful pagoda built, which is still standing today.

Okay, so it wasn't all pomp and rigidity and unfulfilled lives in the forbidden city. There was occasionally a bit of fun when someone got married or had a birthday. Tet (New Year) and fifth month celebrations involved games, ceremonies, music and plays. A princess almost inevitably married beneath herself, which is why her marriage was called a 'descent'. Who was it who said 'I married beneath myself – all women do'? Her fiancé might be a count, a low-grade mandarin or a courtier but rarely a prince. It was hard for a princess to find a husband for three reasons: (1) Most princes were reluctant to marry someone on arrangement, sight unseen. What if she was old and ugly? They would lose face. (2) During mourning periods, which were very long, no weddings were allowed. If a princess endured a few funerals in her teenage years, she risked being too old and ugly, thus missing the boat. (3) A royal wedding cost so much that they couldn't afford to have more than one a year. Say a suitable husband was found for a princess, who had to be over the age of 13 and definitely not fat, 40 and finished. He was given huge amounts of money and a separate palace, his parents turned up at the purple city to kowtow, the astronomy department was called in to set the dates and the papers were signed. Amazing gifts were exchanged such as buffaloes, pigs, wine, betel nuts, linen, silk, laces of pearls and wedges of gold and silver. The princess received instruction from her mother as to her wifely duties, the betrothal took place amid ostentatious pomp and ceremony, the bride and groom arrived at their new home separately and went to two different rooms. I think they got together about nine days later, having never seen each other before in their lives, and lived happily ever after.

Strolling through the once heartbreakingly magnificent, blue-blooded compound where all this happened is a poignant experience rather than an interesting one. What the French and later the Vietcong didn't destroy, the Americans and South Vietnamese bombed the hell out of in the famous Tet Offensive of 1968. You still have to be careful where you walk as there are undetonated bombs. Signs warn you to stick to the marked paths. All that's left are foundations, partially restored buildings, some fabulous gates, two pools and people tending vegetables in the dust.

In 1885 the Nguyen emperor Ham Nghi stood up to French control and, for his trouble, French forces encircled the imperial city and attacked with ruthless savagery, taking three days to steal everything of value and burn the priceless imperial library. The French exiled and replaced the naughty rebellious emperor with the more manageable Dong Khanh. He was succeeded by Thanh Thai who was succeeded by Duy Tan who was succeeded by Khai Dinh whose son, the emperor Bao Dai, was the friend of Alice, whom we met in Ha Long Bay. By the time Bao Dai succeeded the throne, he was leading a puppet regime. During the First World War he abdicated in favour of an 'associated state' with the French government and accepted a post as 'Supreme Adviser'. When Ho Chi Minh took Saigon, Bao Dai was exiled to France where he continued

HUE COM SEN
PERFUMED STICKY RICE

The large amount of pepper is not a mistake. The pork is meant to be suffused with the aromatic taste of fresh pepper (Vietnamese if possible). The lotus leaves for wrapping the rice are from the beautiful water lily and give the rice its balancing yan. If you can't get hold of any, use aluminium foil.

Serves 4–6

vegetable oil
230 g (8 oz) pork, cubed
2 garlic cloves, chopped
2 tsp freshly ground black pepper
2 tbsp nuoc mam
$^1/_2$ tsp sugar
1 cup water
150 g (1 cup) dried lotus seeds, soaked for at least 6 hours
2 lotus leaves (banana leaves will do)
4 cups of cooked sticky rice

1   Make sticky rice – recipe opposite.
2   To cook the pork, heat a little oil in a small pot and briefly sauté the pork and garlic. Add pepper, nuoc mam, sugar and water. Reduce the heat and simmer till tender – about an hour.
3   Drain and cook lotus seeds in salted water for about 5 minutes till tender.
4   Dip lotus leaves in water and trim into 2 large squares. Divide rice into 4 and lay 2 portions in the middle of each leaf – about 10 cm (4 in) square. Shred the pork on top and drizzle over a bit of the cooking juice. On top of this sprinkle the lotus seeds, then cover with the remaining rice, enclosing everything.
5   Fold over the sides of the leaf, making a neat package and secure with string. Steam in a bamboo steamer for half an hour.

To serve: Place on the table, cut leaf open with scissors and invite your guests to dive in.

Makes 4 cups
400 g (2 cups) sticky rice
22 cm (9 in) bamboo steamer
piece of cheesecloth, about 30 cm (12 in) square

1   Cover the rice in 3 times the amount of water and leave to soak in the fridge for 6 hours or more.
2   Drain the rice and rinse in cold water. Place the cheesecloth-lined steamer over a pot of water and bring to the boil.
3   Put the rice on the cheesecloth, fold the edges over and place the lid on. Steam for 25 minutes.

his profligate life. When the North Vietnamese Communists entered they flew their flag from the emperor's tower and in the next three weeks murdered, by very gross methods, 3000 'unsympathetic' people in Hué. Enter the Americans and South Vietnamese who got rid of the Communists by flattening Hué and brutally killing about 10,000 more people, most of them civilians. The Americans said, 'We had to destroy the city in order to liberate it.'

The strange survivor of the destruction of royal life is the cuisine. Cuisine is always the last thing to go – long after language, dress, music and culture. People continue to remember and keep their families together with the food their forebears cooked. Since doi moi, more and more people are opening up their private mansions to reservation-only guests for a set meal of imperial cuisine. My prediction is that this will save the art from disappearing altogether. We took Thierry's advice and booked a dinner chez Y Thao Garden restaurant. The typhoon passing close by Vietnam ensured torrential rain and there's nothing more pleasant than sitting on a beautiful terrace of traditional Vietnamese architecture, protected and surrounded by tasteful furnishings in musky pink and royal blue, listening to the warm rain. Our hostess and the owner of the gracious, two-storeyed home was Madame Cuc, an exquisite, well-bred woman with short dark hair, dressed in a dark aubergine velvet and silk ao dai. She wore a solid silver necklace, high heels, spoke only French and was the diametric opposite of the public relations savvy Madame Ha at Tinh Gia Vien. I ordered some vang rouge, which I find perfectly adequate, but Tanah espied the burgundies on the side table and we began tasting them by the glass.

The first course arrived in the guise of a peacock made from a little pineapple lit from the inside by tiny candles. Into it were stuck Lilliputian spring rolls on toothpicks, delicate and light as feathers. The next dish was a sweet vegetable soup in a dainty bowl, followed by steamed giant prawns. The waitress squeezed lime juice into salt for us to dip them into. Meanwhile the typhoon seemed to be getting closer as thunder smashed overhead, lightning zapped around us and the garden appeared to be filling with water. But what did we care? A deep-fried crepe filled with pork, mushrooms, vegetables and bean sprouts had arrived, to be dipped into sesame, shrimp and peanut sauce. This was followed by a very finely sliced banana flower salad garnished with shrimp crackers and topped with a ground dust of peanut, sesame seed and dried shrimp. Slices of roast duck were quietly placed in front of us, accompanied by a stunning, perfumed rice dish studded with lotus seeds and nuts, which had been steamed in lotus leaves. Everything about this food was fresh, refined and restrained and the atmosphere was calm and refreshingly free of imperial red and black. In another room Madame Cuc's daughter was playing the piano and you felt you were in a languid tropical scene waiting for a man in a cream linen suit to enter stage left, drenched, and say, 'I've spent all night looking for you.' At the end Madame Cuc placed flowers in a vase on the table and offered us dolly cups of lotus tea. The flowers, which looked like fruits on twigs, were made of yellow lentil paste, painted to resemble fruit and dipped in agar-agar. Our payment for the meal was placed in Madame's yellow Louis Vuitton bag. We waded mid-calf deep in water to our taxi outside, accompanied by umbrella-bearing staff, the piano fading in the background.

We liked Hué even though it's a faded glory and there's a slight undercurrent of dissatisfaction in the people. It has a quiet grace, especially on the north bank with the ancient citadel, fortifications and imperial mausoleums. Although it was an important cultural, intellectual and historical city, it has never really recovered from its violent past and there is resentment that more money has not been spent preserving the architectural landmarks. Recently, however, the tombs and citadel were included on an international list of endangered sites so the government has pledged to spend US$1 million on conservation with the help of UNESCO and other foreign organisations. Part of the problem is that the Communists fought long and hard to get rid of the royalist traditions and now they are being asked to restore the buildings they had so gleefully destroyed. But the tourist dollar has spoken and they now see the economic wisdom in not losing the past.

Next stop for us was the 15th-century ancient trading port of Hoi An. Would it be as beautiful and tranquil as Hué? And, more importantly, could it possibly offer better delicacies?

4

Hoi An

Hoi An isn't very far from Hué so we hired a taxi to take us there. This was the best car ride I had in Vietnam as the car was very new and the driver actually knew how to drive. He had all sorts of kitsch American tapes which we played and sang along to as we drove through the Marble Mountains. We stopped at every shrine and lit incense, visited the Linh Ong Pagoda and admired the beautiful scenery. You cannot drive cars into the UNESCO-designated old part of Hoi An so normally the taxi stops outside the ancient city walls and you walk or get carried in on a tuktuk. This is the only place in the whole of Vietnam where cars are forbidden and it's absolute heaven. We had tea with our driver outside the walls, bade him farewell and sank into the tuktuks, which deposited us outside our hotel. We could see immediately that Vinh Hung I fitted all the criteria of charm and grace; all that remained was to manipulate the situation so we got the best rooms. Two of them were 'especially fabulous' and famous for their antique Chinese decor and I was determined to get my hands on one of them. This is the tricky thing about all hotels all over the world: there are ignoble rooms and noble rooms, sometimes they cost the same price and the staff don't care either way, so it's up to you to check them out.

Vinh Hung I was an ancient Chinese trading house, all engraved ebony and lanterns on the outside and pink-washed walls on the inside. Large central doors and two big black french doors on either side opened the hotel up to a wide porch and the street. The lobby had Chinese paintings, lanterns, gold engraved pillars, cabinets full of statues and precious objects and inlaid black furniture softened with red satin cushions. We spent many hours on those cushions, sipping the jasmine tea that was always ready and hot for anyone who desired it, gossiping with the staff in French and English and cooling down under the fans. The night staff slept under a mosquito net on a foam mattress on the floor, ready to open the locked door for latecomers. With promises of better things to come, we settled into two ordinary rooms, complete with multiple insurance showers, and wandered out into the sultry heat to discover our new home for the next few days. Hoi An is a pretty little port town with a fabulous beach and rivers. In one of those fortuitous quirks of geography, this town remained relatively unscathed during the French occupation and American war because shipping operations were moved to nearby Da Nang which, along with the capital, Hué, took the full brunt of the fighting. So Hoi An still looks as it did hundreds of years ago when it was a trading port. Everything has been preserved and protected by UNESCO and the people are proud to live in the tranquillity and stability of this otherworldly place.

Architecturally, Hoi An is a romantic amalgam of the trading communities who have passed through – Dutch, Portuguese, Chinese and Japanese. There's a beautiful little ancient Japanese bridge and the most wonderful Chinese trading houses, still lived in by the descendants of the original owners and open to the public at certain hours of the day. Within half an hour of being in Hoi An I came to the conclusion I couldn't stay there for just two days. Tanah felt the same way and we decided to remain as long as we could. Around the corner from the hotel and across the river is an island that is quite different from the rest of Hoi An. It's like a rural village of poor people all of whom seemed to be smoking dope. The sweet, pungent smell of it hung on the air and every time I turned down another muddy street, there was someone offering me some. The inhabitants of this village acted as if they had never seen a foreigner before. Excited giggling children mobbed me, trying to touch my hair, and people leaned out of their houses, waving and saying hello. A girl in leopard-skin pants and high heels sailed by with the baby and the shopping balanced on her bicycle. Most of the houses were simple bamboo and wood affairs but some people had obviously sold lots of the local product and had spiffy new two-storey studios with shiny tiles and sparkling, electrified shrines. I was desperate to buy one of these flashing altars for my statue of the Virgin (nothing like a spot of cross-cultural spirituality) but couldn't imagine it with the dignified smudgy blue and sage green decor at home.

A woman in the regulation black pyjama pants and man's shirt was holding a chicken's slit neck over a cup to collect the blood, leading me into all sorts of reveries on the food chain. By having eliminated the killing and preparing phase from our first world lives, are we missing out on the connection between life, food and death? When you see a Vietnamese woman sending a chicken to heaven, you're witnessing the culture, the life of the family, the symbolism of religious feasts, culinary achievement and survival. Although chicken is the most popular meat after pork, it also goes with every festive or important occasion and is evidence of the village's wealth. To honour a guest, you kill and cook a chicken; to make an offering to the gods, you use a chicken with its head raised; to feed 60 people, you slice a chicken as thin as moth wings; to do your daughter proud for her wedding, you choose the strongest chicken with the cockiest attitude. All Vietnamese chickens are free range and have to fend for themselves so they're firm to the teeth. You can buy battery-raised birds but the Vietnamese can't stand them — too soft and tasteless. If you want to describe a person as clumsy, you say 'he can't tie a chicken'. If you think he's gullible, you say 'he can't tell the difference between a quail and a chicken'. I, for one, don't have this relationship with the chicken I eat. I buy this naked, white thing in the organic butcher, eat it with tarragon and lemon, groan over its succulence and feel no connection with God, country or flag.

At a café on the river looking back to Hoi An, I met Miss Ruthless. In the technique of working a room, this child had nothing to learn. I was trying to sip my beer without contaminating it with salt from my sweat, the staff of young girls had joined me at my table watching me write and everyone wanted to find out how my hair got like that. Mouths were open, spellbound, as I did the ritual of the lip liner, then the lipstick with the help of the little silver, magnified mirror I carry around with me. The mirror was passed around the whole café then respectfully given back to me. Very beautiful, madame. You very modern, madame. One girl confided in me that although she had two children, she had no husband and didn't want one and what would my marital situation be? How many children? How old? I spat all this information out for the hundredth time. I said I had a husband once but didn't feel the pressing need for another one, although I'm not against them per se. She gave me the thumbs up sign and shared this information with the men in the room. They laughed. When I left, I gave her the silver mirror.

I shooed all the sellers of rubbish away as they came by my table but I couldn't shake Miss Ruthless.

'You buy coins, lady.'

'No thanks.'

'You buy coins, lady.'

'No thanks.'

She stood right next to my face and slapped the old coins tied onto string on the table where I was writing.

'I do you deal for 30,000 dong.'

'No thanks.' I pushed them aside and kept writing. She stood there. I sighed.

'Okay, I'll take two coins for 10,000.'

'No, 30,000.'

'Don't be so outrageous.' I threw up my hands and showed the whites of my eyes.

'Okay, special price 20,000.'

'10,000.'

'20,000.' Face like a can-opener. You could have cracked wood over her nose and she wouldn't have blinked. She never smiled during this whole transaction.

'Christ! I don't even want them. All right, here's 20,000.'

She took the money, quickly folded it into her purse and moved on to wipe out some Germans. She was about five years old.

By now it was early evening and I sauntered on down the river, turned earth-red from the flooding, to the market. The Hoi An market, which is partially under cover, exuberantly swallows you up and explodes as you walk into it. It is very pretty with an over the top, happy, ribald feel to it, unlike any other market I had visited — it was hot, gregarious, relaxed, engaging and rich. In fact Hoi An is doing so well that property prices have increased 200 per cent in the last two years. The people have a different personality from other Vietnamese because they haven't been bombed; they exist in a time warp and I guess I'd be happy too if I lived in an open museum. The stall holders were hilarious, talking to me and hugging and grabbing me all the way through as I took in the huge pots of steaming eggs, all sorts of potatoes, curly eggplants, finger bananas, tables piled with greens, banana blossoms and tofu. The sweet smell of pickled bamboo and herbs permeated everything and as the light faded, the bulbs and candles from the shrines turned the space into a fairyland. At the end of the market closest to the river, the remains of the fish catch lay in bowls and plates on wooden boxes. Even the tiniest fish were filleted, scaled, cleaned and artistically arranged in circles and rows. This work is done even if the fish is bought within seconds, over and over again, as if for a king's household. There's never any question of not working to perfection.

When I went back the next day tiny eggplants were drying in the sun; old people were squatting, playing cards on a sheet of plastic; boys on bikes carrying huge double baskets of the famous golden cao lau noodles were delivering them to various stands; and bottles of snake wine with the snakes in them sat in the sun. Some people were conked out on tables and benches in the gruesome meat department, some cooked the Hoi An version of happy crepes, shredded tobacco leaves were drying on sticks and

FRIED EGGPLANT

Serves 1

1 round white eggplant about the size of a large orange
vegetable or peanut oil
1 sliced spring onion
1 tsp grated garlic
$1/_2$ tsp chopped fresh chilli
$1/_2$ tsp brown sugar
$1/_2$ tbsp soy sauce
2 tbsp lime juice

1   Slice the eggplant thinly to halfway down so that it is still intact. Turn it around and slice the other side, the opposite way. It is still intact.
2   Soak eggplant in salted water for 15 minutes.
3   Boil for 3 minutes in fresh water, holding the eggplant down with a heavy plate.
4   Drain and squeeze the eggplant flat and dry between two weighted plates.
5   Heat a couple of tablespoons of oil in a frying-pan and cook till crispy, about 3 minutes on each side.
6   In another pan, quickly sauté the spring onion, garlic and chilli, then throw in the sugar, soy and lime juice.

To serve:
Place the eggplant on a warmed plate and pour the hot sauce over.

sheets of banana leaves were stacked high. A wonderful girl on the betel leaf stand explained to me how the leaves are chewed, pointing all the while to her grandmother who obligingly gaped her black-stained smile to demonstrate the effects. There are three parts to the preparation: the nut, the leaf and lime. The fresh nut, which is the fruit of the areca tree, is peeled, trimmed at both ends and quartered lengthwise. The leaf, which comes from the piper vine, is cut in half along the centre line. The lime is an alkaline white powder residue which results from cooking coral over a very hot fire for several days. It is violently fiery. Right, now to put the ingredients all together for chewing. Partially coat the inside of the leaf with the lime, roll it up and poke the stem into the leaf to secure it. Next, take a small mortar and put the rolled leaf and a quarter of the nut in and pound with the little pestle for about two minutes until you get a dark red paste. You put this prickly, hot, red stuff in your mouth and chew for about five minutes. Regular users do this about ten times a day and it makes them feel slightly stoned and tranquil.

The market sells tea boxes made of cinnamon wood and you see a lot of cinnamon bark for sale. The Quang Nam province, where Hoi An is situated, was always rather beautiful because of all the cinnamon trees planted in their forests and mountains. It also smelled gorgeous. If you go up to a cinnamon tree, all you have to do is scratch the bark with your fingernail, sniff it and you'll get the message. Cinnamon was used as a yardstick for the wealth of a family and revered through music festivals and art exhibitions as the symbol of a well-bred woman. The trees used to be planted in spring by newly-weds so they would have income from the bark in their old age and by the parents of newborns for the same reason. This spice was so valuable it was used as a currency to buy motor cycles, food and high-grade consumer goods. The leaves and small branches are ground to make incense sticks and the bark is dried and rolled into sticks as a musky aromatic flavouring for both savoury and sweet dishes. It also has medicinal purposes and is used as a perfume.

Then, because of their great value on the export market, farmers began growing cinnamon trees in plantations and almost exploited them out of existence. The tree takes 15 years to mature and is harvested only once so when the bark has been taken the tree dies. The people just kept cutting them down and soon all the pretty domestic gardens full of cinnamon trees were wild and barren. By 1993 the region only had 700 hectares of young trees left. Now, however, things are starting to change. The state has invested in planting cinnamon forests and encouraging villagers to plant domestically. At the moment there are over 4000 hectares in production and a kilo of dried bark fetches more than

VND300,000 or US$20. When I got home I put my black China tea in its tissue-paper wound knots into a cinnamon box and sure enough, after a few weeks, the tea was pleasantly redolent of spice. Very nice with Marmite on toast.

Outside the market there are lots of food stalls serving 'mixed' lunches for the people coming in from fishing trips. Many different things are laid out and you put a bit of everything on your plate. I sat down on the low stool and asked the woman serving to feed me. I got rice, sliced barbecued pork, pickled cabbage, hard-boiled eggs, tofu, sautéed morning glory greens, little grilled fishes, boiled intestines and nuoc cham fish and tomato sauce. They watched me intently, calling people who spoke a bit of English to come over and interrogate me, then gave me a glass of the best water I've ever tasted. Because the river water is too salty to drink, the only fresh water in Hoi An comes from deep wells and is unbelievably cool and sweet. They keep it in portable cool boxes and anyone can take a glassful as they pass by. Speaking of the well water brings me to cao lau noodles which are so good, people say, because they're made with water from a certain square well in Hoi An called the Ba Le. I made a pilgrimage to this well in an alleyway called Phan Chu Trinh, expecting it to be the Holy Grail and UNESCO protected with flashing lights, but it was just in someone's backyard with a plastic sheet over it.

A remnant of the Japanese presence in Hoi An, cao lau noodles are based on soba noodles. You can get them only in Hoi An and they have been made by the same family for over 100 years. They don't just buy rice flour to make the noodles; they rinse, husk, polish and dry the rice themselves, adding ash water during the drying process, which turns the flour the yellow colour that distinguishes these noodles from all others. The process is a bit like that for choux pastry in that it's a hot dough, worked in a banana leaf-lined double-boiler called a xung. They roll the dough out and cut the thick noodles by hand. In restaurants cao lau noodles are always served the same way – reheated in boiling water and placed in a bowl with pork grilled in nuoc mam, bean sprouts, fresh herbs and sliced onion. This is doused with lime juice and soy sauce and garnished with crunched up rice crackers called banh da. The noodles are slightly sour to eat but very satisfying as they're so fat and juicy.

Once again I kept my eye out for pho. Although I didn't see much of the northern style soup in Hoi An, there were lots of other soups that resembled pho but with different names and different ingredients. The two things that were similar were the noodles and the broth. Then all sorts of things like congealed slices of blood, offal of all descriptions, sausages, fish, seafood, sour vegetables or eggs might be added. They also added fragrance with other sauces like Worcestershire, soy sauce, hoisin, tamarind, squid ink or garlic.

On our second day we passed the most beautiful funeral in the world. We thought at first it must have been a funeral parlour but as the week went by and the family were still mourning, Tanah got into conversation with them and they explained that this was their home and the funeral lasted many days. Everyone was dressed in white with white headbands. The candle-lit room contained the body of the deceased, in front of which was a shrine with offerings and incense. The walls were highly decorated with red velvet hangings dripping with yellow fringing and family members and friends sat outside at tables sipping tea. It was the mother who had died and her adult sons were inconsolable as they kept pouring out rice and tea for her. We sat down with them every day, lit incense and bowed three times, drank tea while the brothers told us how wonderful she was and accepted the pieces of red paper they gave us in gratitude for our attention to their mother. One day the white people were gone, the house was back to normal and we knew her soul had been permitted to leave her body.

I've now been upgraded, up the steep old stairs, to the 'especially fabulous' room and write, glowing, on the long, ebony, Chinese-lanterned balcony outside my window, overlooking the pretty street below. There's nothing like the noise of Hanoi here, just general village clatter, mournful singing somewhere, the street-cleaning truck doing its spraying round and even though cars are forbidden, unfortunately hondas are not. My opulent room is immense with two curtained double beds, hat stands, dressing tables, elaborate wall mirrors, desks, cane chairs, ornate shuttered windows and all the wood in black ebony or imitations of it.

It's midnight and a giant cockroach has just sauntered across my bedroom floor. What I really need to know is, do they crawl over you at night? Or do they only go where food is? Is a human food? How can I turn the fact that there is a vile, black, indestructible bush-pig-insect 2 metres from me into an exotic, provocative, gastro-travel experience? Another thing. I know what happens when the light goes off – the rest of its mates turn up to party. If there's anything a big old cockroach loves, it's darkness. Not even a nuclear bomb can kill them and I have one as a sleeping partner. Is this the best I can do? Why am I always walking on the wild side, where is my mother and why is there no God? A few geckos run up the wall but geckos don't bother me, spiders don't bother me, cockroaches make my blood clot.

There's something interesting about geckos. Do you know how they manage to race up and down smooth vertical surfaces, hang upside-down over my bed and support their entire body with one single toe? It's not glue. It's millions of tiny little hairs called setae. A seta is 100 micrometres long and each seta ends with 1000 even tinier pads at the tip. One seta can lift the weight of an ant, a million setae could lift a 20-kilo child and a gecko using all of its setae at the same time could support 125 kilos. These things should be carrying my suitcase. It's geometry, not chemistry – the tiny pads work through a molecular attraction. Geckos' feet never get dirty and researchers think the adhesive is self-cleaning.

To make sure they have a street party every month, the good folk of Hoi An celebrate the full moon (the 14th day of every lunar month) on 'Hoi An Legendary Night'. All traffic is banned from 6 p.m. onwards and as soon as it is dark, all lights in the town go off and it is lit only by lanterns, incense and candles. Everyone comes out onto the street to play and sing and walk arm in arm like a huge passegiata. In the doorway of every establishment, be it hotel, bike shop, home or restaurant, a table is set up with offerings of food and incense to Buddha. The moon was violently bright and old men, dressed in traditional black costume, played chequers in the street while in a little square people were shrieking with laughter around the Vietnamese version of 'pin the tail on the donkey'. Villagers are blindfolded with a wicker mask, then have to try and knock a ceramic pot full of sweets off its high stand with a stick. When someone succeeds the crowd screams dementedly. Feeling hungry, we strolled down to the waterfront to see if we could squeeze into a restaurant. Mistake. Riverfront dining meant (a) relentless hassling by children selling things and (b) being privy to perhaps the most discordant, ghastly concert of traditional singing we had yet heard. The upside was watching little red and white packets of lit candles bobbing down the river like fireflies on a magic carpet.

The 'yoke food' carried around the streets in pots is great in Hoi An. The yoke is one of the oldest methods of transporting food — and babies, vegetables for market, bricks for building sites, fertiliser for fields. The don ganh yoke is a long wooden or bamboo pole with baskets hanging from either end. Sometimes it's carried on one shoulder and sometimes it's balanced across the back of the neck and held with the hands. Both men and women use it and they move in what I call 'the yoke gait', not so much walking as gently bouncing in a fluid movement to protect the back. Although the loads can be very heavy, carriers can turn and slide in and out of crowds very quickly and gracefully. Yoke food can be baguettes, fruit, spring rolls, various snacks and, best of all, whole meals like soups and stews. When you indicate that you'd like to buy some, the person carefully bends the knees to a squat, back straight, and eases off the yoke. My favourite was an old woman who stopped every morning outside the hotel and sold her dish, banh beo, to the staff who adored it and called it country pancakes. Soon I came to adore it too — flat, white discs made from rice flour, yeast and sugar and set in a mould and steamed. These she topped with warm shrimp sauce, fried shallots and broken prawn crackers. Imagine someone coming around your neighbourhood selling such refined delicacies! And what about the ice cream man? He had a fine bicycle complete with parasol and silver box marked 'ICE CREAM'. When he rang his bell, you came running.

I bought a pass to visit one of the 'old houses' and stepped through the doorway protected by the watchful eye – a piece of wood with the am and duong (yin and yang) symbol – into the past. These large, long, two-storeyed buildings are a unique way of experiencing what life was like in the early 19th century and are listed as first rank cultural and historical vestiges. Most of them are double-ended, in the sense that they open onto the street at the front and onto the river at the back. Social life was conducted from the front door and trading business was done directly from sailing ships through the huge back doors. This house was very beautiful and in good condition, with incredible Vietnamese, Japanese and Chinese design in ebony and jack fruit wood. The antique furniture, wall murals and hangings, and the crockery, such as teapots and ceramic bowls, were all authentic. In the main room were two fabulously ornate shrines – one on the left for Buddha and one on the right for the ancestors.

The middle of the house opened up to a roofless courtyard, then continued on, covered, to the kitchens, dining rooms and service area. The lovely courtyard contained a mango tree, a well and an ancient blue and yellow mosaic wall. The upstairs balconies, hung with lanterns, led to what were once storage rooms, but are now used by the family as bedrooms. The owner of the house, a tiny, skinny 80-year-old gentleman with sparkling eyes, had been a teacher and spoke good English. He told me all the generations since his great-grandfather had been born in this house. He explained why the floor was higher than in previous times. All the houses on the river used to flood for three days every year like clockwork; no one thought to question it, it was just nature and had to be accepted. All the precious furniture was put upstairs till the floors dried out. Now the floors have been raised and are not made of wood but of slate. The roof was composed of alternating yin and yang tiles in concave and convex shapes which fitted perfectly together like a man and a woman. If you stood on the balcony outside my especially fabulous room, you could see these ancient rooftops with their emerald green moss coats nourished by the rain.

It was still full monsoon season and raining on and off. When it really rained the electricity went off. These moments invariably occurred when you were at the Internet café pouring your heart out to a faraway lover over perpetual tiny cups of tea. Just as you got to the end of a long e-mail, everything would disappear, never to be retrieved, there would be a loud collective groan from all the other hapless tourists and the café would be vacated in seconds. The Vietnamese would smile placidly in their indifferent calmness and order another pot of tea. Vietnam wins the prize for having the cheapest but slowest e-mail in the world. Out into the hot rain where all Europeans looked exhausted, round-shouldered, sticky, red-faced, cloggy and slack-eyed as if they were only just functioning. They looked as if they were in deep psychological and physical shock and the skimpy, inappropriate beachwear on their doughy white bodies was revolting. The Vietnamese looked slim, cool and brown. But enough about the rain and more about the food.

We signed up for a cooking lesson with Ms Vy (pronounced Vee) at the White Lantern restaurant. It is unusual for a woman in Vietnam to use Ms rather than Miss but the cool Ms Vy was no ordinary woman. Vietnam is crawling with redoubtable, steel females wearing velvet gloves. Think of the Western equivalent of an iron maiden, then get the Vietnamese version into your mind – feminine, attractive, quietly spoken, classy and … ordinary in a way. The rich, diamond-encrusted dressmakers get down on the floor and sew with the staff; Vy wore casual cotton clothes and gently ran an empire. Ms Vy was 34 but looked 24 at the most. Her grandparents had the original family restaurant called the Mermaid, then her parents took over and for the first time were faced with foreigners wanting to eat their food. Ten years ago some Russians turned up and Vy was the only one there; they said, 'Feed us.' She had never cooked for foreigners before and there was no such thing as a menu, so she called her father and said, 'What do I do? What do they eat? Come and help me.'

He said, 'I'm too tired to come over. You do it, think of something.'

'No, no,' she cried, 'you must come over and help me.'

He came over to the restaurant. Nobody could communicate with anybody, so he took the Russians into the kitchen and pointed to things. They were delighted and wanted everything, absolutely everything. The meal went very well and a light snapped on in the entrepreneurial Vy's brain. The very next morning she put a sign outside the Mermaid, listing what the customers had eaten the night before – this was their first menu.

'Vietnamese don't use menus. It's like songs. Everyone knows all the dishes and they just ask for what they feel like that day.'

Now Ms Vy has both the Mermaid and the White Lantern, and a hotel. For three days we had played telephone ping-pong with her and every time we set up a cooking class, she cancelled it. On the third day she cancelled at the last minute then phoned back 15 minutes later to say we could join the class after all; they were on their way to the market and we were to come immediately. We dropped everything as ordered, did a quick tour of the market with her and the group, then jumped into tuktuks to be taken back to the White Lantern for the cooking lesson. A demonstration table had been set up; Vy stood behind it and we sat in front. Like a little doll, she explained, in a voice that slightly betrayed how many times she had said these exact words, that Vietnamese cooking is about harmony, yin and yang and the concept of 'the five flavours' – salty, sweet, sour, bitter and hot. Lightness and freshness are the intent and even if a dish is predominantly hot (as in spicy with pepper or chilli) it will never be a one-dimensional affair; it will also be balanced with the other four flavours. Another important facet of Vietnamese cuisine, aside from appearance and smell, is how it sounds and feels in your mouth. There must be the elements of crunchiness, softness, heat and cold, cooling as with bitter melon or stimulating as with lime.

The recipes she taught were really delicious and I learned all sorts of interesting things from her, such as how important it is to use good quality nuoc mam, which should be a clear orange/brown colour; that they always marinate fish and meat for at least 10 minutes before cooking; that shallots, garlic or spring onion are in every single Vietnamese dish; that you should drain the juice out of green papaya salad after tossing with marinade or it loses its crispness; that you can sharpen your knife on the

GREEN PAPAYA SALAD

If you can get hold of a Vietnamese grater, it is the ideal implement for papaya and carrot salads because it grates long, round spaghetti-sized strips rather than short, flat ones. It won't work with a soft papaya.

Serves 4

3 tsp lime juice

1 tbsp nuoc mam

2 tsp brown sugar

freshly ground black pepper

$\frac{1}{2}$ tsp chopped fresh chilli

1 tsp grated garlic

1 green papaya, peeled and julienned

1 small carrot, peeled and julienned

1 cup roasted chopped peanuts

2 tbsp finely sliced red onion

$\frac{1}{2}$ cup chopped mint

$\frac{1}{2}$ cup chopped basil

1   Make the marinade by mixing together the lime juice, nuoc mam, sugar, pepper, chilli and garlic. Toss the papaya and carrot in this, then put your hand over the salad and drain excess liquid off. If you leave it sitting in the marinade, it will go limp.

2   Mix in half the peanuts, the onion and half the mint and basil.

To serve: Place the salad on a plate and top with the rest of the peanuts, mint and basil.

---

back of a plate. I found out why the peanuts are so delicious. They heat sand in a wok till it's very hot then throw the peanuts in and toss them till golden. This gives a gentle, even roast with absolutely no burnt bits and at the end the sand is sieved out.

Now curry soup sounds really boring but don't hesitate to order it when you see it on a menu in Vietnam. It's absolutely smashing and nothing like any curry you've tasted. They got it from Indianised Cambodia, which introduced Indian spices and techniques to Vietnamese cuisine. As with everything they touch, the Viets improved on the original source and because harmony is everything and they found very hot curries invasive and overpowering, they toned them down and added their own spices to balance the soup and give it more aroma. Vegetable curry soup is now made with vegetables such as potatoes, carrots, taro and turnip and flavourings like coconut cream, turmeric, lemon grass and brown sugar.

Vy taught us how to make spring rolls; to stir-fry green beans with garlic, shallots, brown sugar and fish sauce, then top them with fried tomatoes and fresh coriander; to stuff squid with marinated pork; to make crispy noodles with pork, prawns, black mushrooms, tomato and pineapple; and to make the famous green papaya salad. Turmeric marinated tuna, grilled in banana leaves, is a great Hoi An speciality and utterly divine to eat. Vy cubed white tuna and marinated it in turmeric, nuoc mam, garlic, red onion, chilli and brown sugar, then added chopped vermicelli, spring onion and black mushroom. This mixture she plopped into the middle of a banana leaf and made a parcel, then wrapped it in four more leaves, imprisoned the package in the little barbecue frame and grilled it over charcoal. When you opened the leaves up your nostrils were caressed by 'the five flavours' and the taste was very tender, with the smokiness of the charcoal somehow permeating the fish. Fish is often served with a ginger dipping sauce, to neutralise any fishy odours.

But the pièce de résistance, the recipe that blew me away, was Vy's ingenious and original way of cooking eggplant. You have to use the round white eggplant about the size of an orange. You slice it thinly all the way through to halfway down in the direction of the stem, so that it remains intact, then turn it upside-down and rotate it to slice it the other way on the other side. Then it's soaked, boiled, weighted and squashed flat to remove the water, then fried. It's served, meltingly succulent on the inside and crispy on the outside, drenched in a sauce of sautéed spring onion, garlic, chilli, soy sauce and lime juice. Vy assured me this recipe was a family one but to me it really smacked of Française because Vietnamese vegetables are always chopped, never cooked whole, and the business of weighting and cross-cutting seemed almost North African,

TUNA GRILLED IN BANANA LEAVES

Serves 3

1 tbsp nuoc mam

freshly ground black pepper

$1/_2$ chopped fresh chilli

2 grated garlic cloves

30 g (1 oz) chopped red onion

2 tsp fresh turmeric grated or 1 tsp powdered

500 g (1 lb) very fresh tuna, cubed

30 g (1 oz) prepared rice vermicelli (soaked in warm water for 10 minutes)

30 g (1 oz) prepared black Chinese mushrooms (soaked in water for 10 minutes)

30 g (1 oz) finely sliced spring onion

2 tbsp vegetable oil

9 banana leaves

3 small barbecue frames

ginger dipping sauce (recipe opposite)

rice

1   Mix the marinade ingredients of nuoc mam, pepper, chilli, garlic, onion and turmeric together and marinate the tuna in them for half an hour. Add vermicelli, mushrooms, spring onion and oil.

2   To make one, place a third of the tuna mixture in the centre of a banana leaf and wrap up like a parcel. Repeat this with another 2 leaves.

3   Lock into the barbecue frame and grill for 7 minutes on each side. If you don't have a barbecue frame, tie the packets up with string and cook them under the oven grill.

To serve: Place the grilled packet on a plate and allow your guests to open it up themselves. Serve with ginger dipping sauce and rice.

like the cutting of preserved lemons. I never saw another vegetable dish remotely like this the entire time I was in Vietnam.

Another famous and very enchanting dish particular to Hoi An is what they call White Rose. White roses, like cao lau noodles, are made by only

Nuoc Cham Gung
Ginger Dipping Sauce

1 1/2 tbsp sugar
2 cloves of garlic
1 fresh red chilli, chopped
1 tbsp fresh grated ginger
2 tbsp water
3 tbsp lime juice
3 tbsp nuoc mam

Grind the sugar, garlic, chilli and ginger to a paste with a mortar and pestle, then add the water, lime juice and nuoc mam.

one family in Hoi An and they supply all the restaurants. One of the daughters of this family came in and gave us a special demonstration. The 'roses' are constructed from transparent rice flour dough, stuffed and formed into little flowers before being steamed. About eight or nine of them are arranged on a plate in the shape of a rose, then garnished with fried shallots and fresh chives and served with a dipping sauce. It is a very refined, delicate dish suitable for princesses and fairies. This girl made thousands of roses every week. She pinched a smidgen of dough from a big lump and formed a long, thin cap by rolling and shaping it with her fingertips. Into this she stuffed a little shrimp paste, pinched it closed and allowed the excess to flower out like a petal. Some she shaped like tiny Cornish pasties then steamed them for eight minutes in a very fine-holed steamer.

The written recipes were like Madame Mai's at the Metropole cooking class – missing all sorts of important information and ingredients. In Vy's recipe for turmeric tuna grilled in banana leaves, both the turmeric and banana leaves were missing. The advantage was that, because it was a hands on class, we were able to make hopeless white roses and spring rolls that looked like toilet rolls. At the end of the class, we were offered the chance to go home, freshen up and come back at 7 p.m. for dinner. The price for all this was US$10! The other students were part of a gastronomic tour from Melbourne. The guide was an extremely gaunt, tall Vietnamese Australian man with wonderful thick hair that had been dyed orange with 3 centimetres of grey roots showing. The punters assured me he didn't eat but lived on coffee and cigarettes and they found him very charming and helpful. As soon as we sat down at the table and Tanah started going on about her choice of wine, I noticed an expression of glazed acrimony pass over his face. Oh-oh, I thought, either he dislikes his job or he dislikes us. He didn't touch any of the beautiful food we were served and ate a plate of chips instead. He knew about Vietnamese food but was sick of eating the exact same dishes Miss Vy provided every time. In my table conversation with the punters, I discovered that they didn't know what pho was and had not tasted it. This was like being in Italy and saying you had never heard of pasta. They ate Western breakfasts, had not sampled any street food, ate only Vietnamese restaurant food and had never heard of Da Lat vang rouge. They were having a fabulous time and loved the tour.

During dinner we were served spring rolls which we all gobbled up. No sooner had the last bit slid down my gullet than my brain came back from Mars. I leaned over, grabbed the lettuce leaves and herbs and said to my immediate neighbours, 'Oh, I've just remembered how I was taught to eat these things. You're supposed to wrap them up in these herbs and lettuce leaves and dip them.' This I proceeded to do. Suddenly the Michael Jackson of gastronomic tourism stood up, walked to where I was sitting and spat, 'I'm in charge of this tour and if anything needs explaining, I'll do it', strutted out of the restaurant and sucked on a few fags rather than the melting eggplant the rest of us were enjoying.

'What was that about?' I asked Tanah, embarrassed. She who knows the gay world inside out, replied, 'Oh, don't worry about it. He's a bit anorexic, I think, lots of fun on a good hair day but you stood on his toes. Flick it.' Upon his return he had changed personalities and chatted brightly to Tanah for the rest of the dinner, which goes to prove cigarettes are good for you after all.

The next morning we enquired about the best body massage in town, accepted the recommendation of Mr Lan at the front desk and found ourselves in a suburban torture parlour. Everyone was very friendly and polite and we were ushered into a shack, one on each plank, no towels for modesty, curtains instead of a door and the male members of the family wandering around just outside. I know it all sounds desperate but the heat gets to you and you do mad things. Every so often a goliath cockroach would wander in, my body would go into simulated rigor mortis and soundless screaming and the pig-insect would be booted out into the next room. As usual we burst into laughter at our situation and decided to go with the flow. Because everything is so cheap in Vietnam we agreed to have steam facials and masks as well, which went on and on and on as all these beauty treatments do; they value quantity over quality. It only hurt when we laughed.

'I think my mask is made of strawberry jam and formaldehyde. I feel like I've fallen off my bike right onto my face,' said Tanah from her plank.

'Mine feels like it's being pricked by a hundred needles which are slightly blunt. I think I've just had an acid peel for $6 and if I don't look 20 years younger by tomorrow morning, I want my money back. Tanah, are we losing our minds? Have we gone troppo or something?'

She shrieked with laughter. 'No, darl. No more so than usual. It's you and the people. Remember?'

Walking around Hoi An you often hear a loud clackety-clack, clackety-clack in the back of a shop. We wandered into 14 Le Loi Street to discover an ancient world of cotton and silk weaving. Silk making was the closely guarded secret of the Chinese for centuries, ensuring them great wealth, and death to anyone who got too close to the source, but with the collapse of the Tang dynasty in 907, the mystical silk world was revealed for everyone to see. The Vietnamese then became master silk weavers, in places making even finer silk than the Chinese. So there, standing in front of us, was a 17th-century wooden silk loom clacking away. Upstairs, baby white silkworms were squiggling around on a huge, flat bamboo basket in a wire and wooden cabinet. They start their lives off as tiny black dots, sleep for three days then turn white. They eat very finely sliced mulberry leaves every three hours and twice a night for three days then rest for one day while they moult. This goes on for about 16 days till they become an roi or 'devouring' and are moved to a bigger cabinet with larger leaves, freshly replenished by the staff every day.

For eight days they gorge themselves in an orgy of gluttony. When they reach their adult size they carry a full stomach of silk inside their now red bodies. The worms are then placed on fine branches enclosed in a bamboo rack to spin their silvery cocoons. This they do over four days by spitting out the silk thread and winding it round and round their exhausted bodies from the outside to the inside. They are making their protective home, which looks like a little egg, for the moment when they stay inside and turn into a chrysalis. In an ideal world, the chrysalis would now turn into a moth and burrow its way out, lay lots of eggs on a mulberry leaf and the whole natural cycle would begin again. However in the world of silk making, the chrysalises are then murdered inside their cocoons by being boiled in water. You just pick up a cocoon and pull a thread out from the base and it goes on and on and on for 500 metres! This impossibly fine, almost invisible thread is wrapped onto spools, then woven into fabric. It takes 20 kilos of cocoon to produce 1 kilo of raw silvery white silk. When you see how it's made you can't believe it's not more expensive.

Now here's the thing: nothing is ever wasted in Vietnam, so when all the thread is unwound, what do you do with the murdered chrysalises? Why, eat them, of course. I often saw bowls of yellowy-brown, dried insects at the market food stalls and wondered what they were. Now I know — silk chrysalises that have been fried with spices and oil and served with rice. They are also eaten as crunchy snacks with rice wine. The girl at the silk shop explained to me that eating chrysalises is not an exquisite pleasure entirely without danger for they can poison you. The farmers spray the rice, the mulberry trees nearby get contaminated, sometimes the moths die and if the poison is still in the chrysalis, the person who eats it will get sick.

Speaking of silk, Hoi An is famous for its made-to-order clothing shops so, in spite of having been through it before we couldn't resist going through it again. Thu Thuy at 60 Le Loi Street had been recommended as the most expensive but the best. Boy, was she some operator — tiny, about 37, short pixie cut hair, perfect make-up, red nails, dripping diamonds and gold. From the shop, we were ushered out the back to a 90 square-metre area of gardens, workshops, a chic café and rooms lined with every fabric imaginable. Thuy told me she used 100 tailors and had 20 sales girls who all wore the same beautiful outfit, which changed every day. If you go for a week, as we did, you see the whole range of changing colours and outfits. It's like being in a Peter Greenaway movie where, as you walk through different rooms, your dress changes colour to match the decor. They provide you with tea in tiny cups, tell you you are beautiful and ask where your diamonds come from, offer free Internet access and do tough deals with gentle smiles. It was worth getting dresses made just for the relatively efficient e-mail.

First you have to know how to chose fine silk and these are the methods of divination:

(1) Pull the cloth and if the threads stay tight, it is authentic silk. If there's elasticity, the cloth is made from chemical threads.

(2) Burn a piece of cloth. If the ash is loose and smells of burnt hair or plant, it is silk. If not, the ash lumps.

(3) When the cloth is either too easy or too hard to crumple, it is polyester. Silk crumples just a little.

(4) Make your hand cold by holding ice cubes, for example, then put it on the cloth. If your hand gets warm quickly, it's silk.

Having amused myself with some of these secret tests, I then decided on a red Chinese jacket, kimono, a copy of a top I already owned and a black silk dress — but only after Thuy had approved of my choice. They look mercilessly at your body, your skin, your personality and your diamonds to judge what's best for you.

'No, no, no. You can't have that silk ... it's not the right one for that style of dress ... you need this one.'

'No. I want this 100 per cent silk.'

'No, believe me, this silk mix much better.'

'But I want this.'

'No. You take this.'

I did what I was told. Vietnamese are very conservative and it's hard for them to step out of the square. This is the way they've always made garments so this is the way it will be.

'I want longer sleeves.'

'No. Look silly like that. This design must have short sleeves. I stake my career on it. I do this all my life, Peta ... trust me ... I know better.'

'Okay.'

I'll never wear it because the sleeves are too short but c'est la vie. What do I know?

Tanah, with her challenging and voluptuous body, ran circles around them. When it got up to her spending $US500 they allowed her a little leeway. We kept ordering more things and by the end of a week we had them doing outrageous colour combinations like ming blue and lime green kimonos, mauve tops with red buttons, purple pants with turquoise piping, black jackets with red lining. They made us Chinese thongs of all hues, always with the dire warning, 'I can't sell this to anyone else, Tanah and Peta. If you no like when finish, you pay.'

My favourite sales assistant was Dung, affectionately known as Ung-ung, which I couldn't pronounce, so I called her Yum-yum. She was very pretty, had a yearning, wistful nature and often seemed tired. I soon found out why. She would lean on me and say,

'Peta, why I so lazy? Are you lazy? I want lie down all the time.'

'I don't think you're lazy, Yum-yum, I think you're tired. How many hours do you work here?'

'All day, from 8 a.m. to 10 or 11 p.m., seven days a week. I get up at 6 a.m. and my English teacher comes to my home at 6.30. I do an hour of English, a bit of sweeping for my mother, then come here to work.'

'What about fun and boyfriends?'

'I had a boyfriend from Saigon but he no good. Now I looking again but I like single – no trouble when you single.'

'How are you going to meet a boy when you work all the time?'

'I don't know, Peta ... you find me rich husband ... you take me to your country ... I look after you. You look after me.'

If this sounds terrible, I never saw Thuy work many fewer hours than the girls and she was often in there on the floor sewing by hand late at night, although she did take days off and have a sleep occasionally. Her husband is in the business with her, they have a fabulous house and three children who are looked after by her mother and sister.

We fell in love with certain families and individuals in the town. The family who made our favourite cakes, our lampshades, sold our Bordeaux wine and engaged us in intelligent conversation, lived just around the corner from the hotel. Mr Khoi of Bao Ngan shop on Le Loi Street was expected to continue his father's shoe making business but times were very tough after the American war so he and his serene, lovely wife did whatever worked to pay the bills. In general, the family home is also the place of business. In this case what would have been the front salon was the shop and it was open all day from 8 a.m. to 11 p.m. At night they shuttered the shop by inserting horizontal planks into grooves cut into the columns that supported the roof. He sold wine and spirits; she made decorative birthday cakes and what she called 'plain cake', small cupcakes with a raisin on top which I imagine are a derivative of the French quatre quart or pound cake. They had two teenage daughters, then decided they would try for a son and this little creature must have been the most adored boy on the planet. Every time we went to the shop, we sat down for a drink and a natter about the old days and what a good choice of wife Khoi had made. He took Tanah for a sightseeing ride on his honda om; I think it was the experience of his life being so close to such a well-endowed woman.

In appreciation of our custom, bargaining ability and entertainment value, the management of the hotel invited us out to lunch the day before we left. Our witty sparring partner, the redoubtable Lan at the front desk, was chosen to accompany us. He turned up on his bicycle at 1 p.m. sharp in pressed shirt and good shoes instead of sandals, sat through the lunch of Hoi An favourites like cao lau noodles and asparagus and corn soup, engaged us in conversation and never ate a thing. I believe he sneaked downstairs and had a plate of chips. He had a university education, specialising in anything to do with English – culture, business practice and language. We were sitting on the balcony so had a good view of the street. Schoolboys dressed in blue pants, white shirts and caps bicycled by; girls with long black hair down their backs strolled along, conical hats protecting their beautiful skin; an old woman with yoke food crossed the street … oh no! She trips and falls, the steaming hot pork stew pouring all over her bare feet. A day's income gone in a second. She is very upset and sits in the street, staring at the carnage and the broken yoke. Lan jumps up and runs down, other people come out of their houses to help her. They put her in a chair on the footpath, soak her burnt feet in cold water, clean the mess up and get a cart to take her stuff home. She is very quiet, doesn't complain and just looks dejectedly at her empty pots, no doubt thinking of her empty purse.

Doing business in English is the key to the future for Vietnamese but doing business at the post office requires much greater skills. Fortunately Lan took me and my box of stuff to send home, on his honda om. You couldn't do it without a translator; you couldn't do it without a counsellor really. I know it's a worldwide requirement for postal workers to move slowly and ignore you if possible but the Vietnamese have perfected this. On the counter is a list of things you're forbidden to post: anything made of wood, antiques, books, CDs, explosives. First you fill in a form stating every single thing in the box, its value and how many of each thing. There's absolutely no reason to believe you so they unpack everything you've very carefully packed and look at it, open it, remove forbiddens and put it all back in again. I was given back a small knife, thank you very much. Opening the bag of kitchen utensils, dried noodles, carrot scrapers and rice paper, they looked at me sharply and said, 'There's dried shrimp in here.'

'There might be,' I replied. 'Who knows what might be stuck in your bag in a Vietnamese market? Have you checked for cockroaches because they don't allow fresh food into my country.'

Fortunately they thought this was funny so the shrimp were allowed to stay.

Six, count them, six forms later, all of which stated exactly the same thing, my box was accepted.

On Tanah's last evening in Hoi An we discovered a stunning, upmarket restaurant on Phan Boi Chau Street called Brother's Café. The brochure assured us it was 'an ancient house, harmoniously landscaped by an exquisite garden with a masterly and tasteful decoration, offering a peaceful and solemn world by its original unique design'. If that makes no sense, I can assure you, the food did. Even the walk to this restaurant was charming, along quiet streets just beyond the main hustle and bustle. Phan Boi Chau Street runs parallel to the water so we could see right through the two-storeyed houses, which were always open, to the river. In the sultry, quiet evening people were watching TV, eating dinner, playing cards, lying down and playing adoringly with toddlers. Then you stepped into this five-star world where 'by the exclusively original tastes and dining experience, your feelings will be stylised as a part of the local followed by a variety of drinking and dishes offering.' Our feelings were particularly stylised by the exclusively original waiter, who was straight out of central casting, playing the role of the north Chinese lover. He was as I imagined an Oriental hero – languid, refined, handsome; a prince among men. Le's speech was exquisite; he had learnt English from the BBC and spoke with precision and care, as if reciting lines for an audition. His smile was radiant as he repeated everything we said, ordered or dreamed. Italian opera was playing on the sound system, competing with the singing of the frogs and cicadas. We gazed at Le besottedly, relieved from this reverie only by the utterly perfect food. While we dined on delicate, beautifully presented dishes such as asparagus and crab soup, shredded chicken salad, grilled eggplant, calamari salad and perfumed rice in an ornate box, Le wrote in my notebook:

I would like to wish you a spring of hope,
A summer of happiness,
An autumn of understanding
And a winter of wisdom.

The next day, after Tanah had flown home, I took myself off to Ms Vy's Mermaid restaurant toute seule and there they were, making the exact same dishes we had learnt in our cooking class at the White Lantern. I had to have the fried eggplant again and also ordered their wontons which were very unusual – sort of deconstructed but delicious. Instead of being folded into a classic wanton shape, the pastry disc was deep-fried flat and topped with a zingy mixture of chopped fresh tomato, herbs and crab meat. Ms Vy knows everything that's going on in Hoi An, who it's going on with and if anyone interesting has arrived.

When Tanah and I ordered our wine at the cooking class dinner, she had said, 'The Bordeaux de Ginestet you bought last night was better.'

'How do you know?'

'The staff told me you were here, what you ordered and what you drank.'

When I sat down at the Mermaid, the waitress said, 'Oh, I know who you are. Where's your friend. You want some French wine?'

I finished the meal off with yoghurt, introduced to the Vietnamese by the French along with all dairy products. They overcame their natural distaste for eating dairy and now make really good, thick yoghurt. There's nothing more soothing for a dodgy stomach than a pot of rich mango and lemon curdled milk.

Of course I could have stayed in Hoi An forever, writing, cooking and decorating one of the old houses for myself. Before long I would have learnt Vietnamese and turned into a nice person just like them. But Saigon, which both scared and fascinated me, beckoned. I was loath to face a big, dirty, noisy city again after the tranquillity of Hoi An but I had to get to the bottom of the pho story. Had I eaten the best pho yet or was it still to come?

5

Saigon

Riding from the airport into Ho Chi Minh City or Saigon, as most people who live there are starting to call it again if no one from the party is listening, is pretty much like riding into any big, ugly Asian city – noisy, dirty, hot and overcrowded. In fact, it's so filthy that almost everyone on a bicycle or motor bike wears a face mask. HCMC central has dust, sulphur dioxide and carbon monoxide levels 1.2 to 2.5 times higher than the standard level. In the industrial areas it is as high as 3.75.

I had called Alice, whom I met in Ha Long Bay, to see if there was room at her cousin's house in Saigon. There was and I duly arrived. The cousin had been very wealthy before 1975 when the Communists took over but that was more or less finished and she now unofficially rented out rooms to visitors and had a transport business. She had owned numerous big hotels plus the large building next door in what had once been a good area in central Saigon. The building I was in had been taken over by the government and she had been left with the ground and first floor only for her family. Instead of a well-cared for footpath outside her home, there were now derelicts, junkies, a bike fixing set-up, broken pavement and nasty looking street stalls. When Alice and I stepped out for a drink at the Majestic hotel that night, someone threw a corn cob at us.

'It's not very smart to do that to foreigners,' snapped Alice. 'If they don't come here, you'll end up very hungry.' Down the road was a large, tawdry place dominated by the most appalling Soviet looking monument. 'There used to be a beautiful big turtle and lovely gardens there,' sighed Alice.

My room was large but run-down with a rattling, ineffectual air-con, a fridge that didn't work and no top sheet on the bed. When I mentioned the fridge, another one in working order was lugged up the stairs, scrubbed there and then in the room and switched on with a flourish. When I asked for a sheet, the maids were perplexed. I called Alice from my mobile in my room to her mobile in her room, and she said, 'In the summer we don't sleep with a top sheet. We sleep in light clothing on the bottom sheet and that's it.' I remembered the film, *The Scent of Green Papaya*, and it's true, the people in that household slept with no top sheet. Nevertheless I wanted a sheet, so followed the maid into the main house which was completely different from my room. It was sumptuous, beautifully furnished and in very good condition. The two maids slept on one bed in a horrible room next to the kitchen. They never stopped smiling and nothing was too much trouble. When they brought me tea in the morning it was as if it had gold leaf floating in it, so gently did they hand it over. The cousin charged me for five nights when I had stayed four but they couldn't be talked out of it and US$18 was cheap for Saigon anyway so I let it slip. They charged me US$10 for a taxi to the airport when the maximum price is US$5 and I was glad they didn't charge me extra for the giant cockroaches and noise. The cousin was the opposite of Alice, who was generous to a fault.

Out the door and into the busy street to see what I could see. One of the defining images of Saigon street life is the beautiful flying angels — girls dressed in the traditional ao dai, or some other stylish dress, and riding on honda oms. If you're a pillion passenger you sit side-saddle adorned in long gloves, mask, sunglasses, sometimes hat and high-heeled mules or platforms. At night all the extra gear gets dropped except for the mask. If you're riding on your own you sit carefully on the back flap of the dress and grasp the front flap daintily in your left hand on the left handle of the bike. Along with the sari, the ao dai must be one of the most beautiful national dresses ever invented. The original ao dais first came to be worn in 1744 when lord Vu Vuong of the Nguyen Dynasty decreed that both men and women should wear trousers and a gown that buttoned down the front. In the 1920s King Duy Tan modernised the ao dai so that it started to look more as it does today. In 1935 the artist Le Pho made it much more body hugging with a low collar but it wasn't till the 1950s that two Saigon tailors produced an ao dai with long, straight sleeves. This created a diagonal seam running from the collar to the underarm with the buttons along the shoulder and side seam, the style everyone wears today. The pants are fitting at the top and flared at the bottom and the willow-like Saigon girls wear them very long over vertiginously high platform shoes because they all want to be tall.

This sexy, elegant dress is half closed and half open, yin and yang. The gown part is split from the waist on either side, so it accentuates the breasts and the hips (yang) and hides the abdomen and legs (yin). When you walk in an ao dai, it creates a sensual flow of the fabric like a cloud floating along the street. In principle the colour of ao dai you wear tells people how old you are and what your marital status is. School girls wear white, young unmarried women wear pastel colours and married or older women wear rich, strong colours usually over black or white pants. In the north in the 1960s, the ao dai was rejected on the grounds that it was superfluous and not appropriate for hard revolutionary work. This drought lasted till the 1980s and though it's not exactly an everyday dress, it's worn on formal occasions, most schoolgirls wear it and almost all women in the hospitality industry wear it and look stunning. The best place for a visitor to buy a classy au dai or any designer dress in Vietnam is Khai Silk. It's desperately expensive, fabulous and very sophisticated.

Now that I was in Saigon, which reputedly had the finest cooking in Vietnam, I was determined to find the ultimate pho. I had only to turn to my culinary expert Alice but she was way ahead of me.

'I know what you want and we're going to a pho restaurant today. Anything else you have tasted will pale in comparison. I've told you the south does things differently from anywhere else – now you will find out.'

She and another cousin take me to Pho Hoa restaurant on Pasteur Street in district three. The small restaurant is very busy and doing business in the typical speedy Vietnamese way. Before you even sit down you're in love with what is on the table waiting for you. Southern cooks are into abundance and presentation – they want you to gasp before you even start, so I oblige. Alice and the cousin smile placidly; they've had this goodness all their lives and Alice owns Vietnamese restaurants in Paris, for heaven's sake. There's nothing she doesn't know about cooking, and she always takes control and orders extra titbits.

The table is set with a dish piled high with fresh herbs like mint, basil, verbena and coriander, a plate of long thin doughnut bread, cut limes, chillies, a plate of bean sprouts and sauces like hoisin and nuoc mam. Hoisin sauce is Chinese but the Vietnamese use it a lot. It's brown, thick and sticky and made from soybeans, red beans, chilli, sesame oil and garlic. We pop our plastic facecloth bags which they have obviously kept in the freezer. I mop up the river on my face and neck and Alice genteelly pats her nose. Almost immediately large bowls of broth containing beef or chicken and rice noodles are brought to the table, along with extra sliced beef Alice has ordered. It can take up to 24 hours to make a good broth for pho. It's mostly made of shinbones, oxtails and other cheap cuts of meat, vegetables, ginger and star anise. When a Vietnamese recipe calls for stock, it doesn't taste like any other French style stock – it is subtly oriental and fragrant. The cook briefly immerses the noodles in boiling water, then places them in the bowl, pours the broth over them, then places some finely sliced onions and minced ginger on top. Because the cooks keep poaching other things like blood and meatballs in the broth all day, it takes on a fantastic flavour. Pho Hoa pho is irreproachable. It's both elegant and simple, complex and obvious and it satisfies your need for different textures and perfumes as no other dish in Vietnam can. It's Vietnam in a bowl, just as tagine is Morocco in a bowl and smoked salmon and soda bread is Ireland on a plate. We pile our toppings and herbs and bean sprouts into the soup, mix it around and devour with chopsticks in one hand and spoon in the other. Alice fishes out the best bits and puts them in my bowl, a sign that she cares about me and is a good hostess. Just in case you need a palate opener or closer, sitting on the table there are also little mild pork sausages wrapped in banana leaves and little boxes made of leaves stuffed with sticky rice and sweet bean paste called banh phu the. The boss is wandering around with fistfuls of money. That's how it's done in cheap restaurants — you just grab her as she's walking by and pay, and the fact that there are no coins in Vietnamese currency makes it easy.

This was the pho of my dreams. I hate to say it — and it's something I find most mysterious — but the pho in Saigon is better than anywhere else in the country, including the north, whence it came. They've taken what's good and delicious in the north and made it into a gastronomic festival in the south. Southerners say the cooking in the north is rubbish and if it wasn't for them improving their dishes, they would be inedible. Northerners say southern food is full of sugar and spices and you can't taste anything. Either way, I found out from a chef in Saigon that everybody all over the country loads everything with monosodium glutamate. This surprised me because, apart from thirst, I hadn't really noticed the effects of MSG and don't understand why they use it; they certainly don't need to. Pho is such an addictive dish because it has everything in it you need to be happy forever, over and over again. Isn't that what we want? Never to get tired of things, to love them multiply and orgasmically as if it were the first time? Don't we want epicurean poetry?

One of the more esoteric experiences I had with Alice was our visit to the one-dollar massage parlour. One afternoon her Vietnamese friend Françoise, the party girl and restaurant manager with the surgically

Pho Bo
Beef Noodle Soup

Serves 6

To make the broth:

1.5 kg (3 lb) oxtail, chopped into pieces

1.5 kg (3 lb) beef shanks

4 l (7 pints) water

3 thumb joint pieces fresh ginger, unpeeled

1 large onion, cut in half and unpeeled

4 shallots, unpeeled

500g (1 lb) daikon (Chinese radish) or turnip in chunks

3 carrots (about 350 g/12 oz) unpeeled in chunks

4 star anise

6 cloves

1 cinnamon stick

1 tsp salt

1 tsp black peppercorns

$1/4$ cup nuoc mam

1   Place the water, oxtail and beef shanks in a large stockpot, cover and bring to the boil.

2   Meanwhile turn the grill onto high, place ginger, onion and shallots on an oven tray and brown on all sides for about 5 minutes. The Vietnamese say this is the secret to a good broth.

3   When the water comes to the boil, skim the scum off with a wire skimmer or spoon. Keep doing this for about 10 minutes till the surface is clear of all foam.

4   Add the browned vegetables and everything else except the nuoc mam, bring the broth to the boil then reduce to a simmer. Cover and simmer for at least 3 hours, longer if you have time.

5   When the broth has cooled, strain it through a chinois (fine sieve) and discard the solids (I eat them with Dijon mustard). Let stand in a cool place till the fat has risen to the surface then skim it off. Add the nuoc mam and taste for seasoning.

The accompaniments of noodles, beef and garnishes:
500 g (1 lb) dried, flat rice sticks
300 g (10 oz) beef round in one piece about 7 cm (3 in) thick
1 large onion
2 spring onions (scallions)
2 small fresh red chillies
handful of bean sprouts
a bunch of fresh coriander (cilantro)
a bunch of fresh mint
2 limes, cut in wedges
nuoc mam

1   Soak noodles in warm water till soft – about 20 minutes. Drain and put aside.
2   Cut the beef across the grain into paper-thin slices. I often put the meat in the freezer for half an hour first to make it easier to slice.
3   Slice onion, spring onion and chillies very finely and place in 3 separate bowls.
4   Dip the noodles in rapidly boiling water for about 30 seconds and drain.

To serve: Divide noodles among 6 deep soup bowls. Top with some slices of beef, some onions and shallots, a few chillies and some bean sprouts. Ladle hot broth over the top. Garnish with herbs and serve with lime wedges. Add nuoc mam to taste.

enhanced breasts and face, turned up with her girlfriends in a huge four-wheel drive. When they saw me they all looked at each other then said, 'We can't take your friend, Alice. We daren't. It's too downmarket for her.'

'Absolute rubbish,' I said, 'wild horses wouldn't keep me away.'

I was dressed in a black dotty skirt and shocking pink top and Alice was her usual chic self. She must be 60 something and there she was in capri pants revealing great legs, high-heeled mules, fitting jacket, designer handbag and the black hair in the ever perfect French roll. We all piled in and, to the accompaniment of the Gypsy Kings, were driven by the chauffeur to some steamy outfit in a sordid back street. There in a large room the six of us removed all our clothes except our knickers and lay down on tables communally, as it were, to be pulled, swished, flicked, cracked, banged, slapped and rubbed into oblivion. Some women also had a breast and tummy massage. It was a room full of women rearranging other women. The masseuses were dressed in pale grey smocks and mine had a voice like a tinkling bellbird. The room was full of gossip and giggling and every so often someone would burst into song. It was so cheap we all had a double session of an hour and a half. Alice's judgement of this place was that the massage was good but she didn't appreciate the ambience. On the way home a honda drove into our car, but both parties just drove off, not even working up enough interest to check out any damage. When I think of how hysterical we are in the West about road accidents it makes me laugh.

In Vietnam there's no such thing as making an appointment; if you want to do something you just turn up. So at six o'clock on one torpid evening Alice and I decided to go to the beauty parlour. She could be a bit mercurial and vague and had a Vietnamese sense of time, so even though it was only around the corner, we walked around in circles and didn't get there till seven. The salon was modern and upmarket, with chic white and black decor, groovy staff and boy, was it was pumping. They shampooed my hair in the chair – so they were doing something wet in a dry area which, as an ex-nurse, I knew you could go to hell for. They were not mean with the head massage as in the West either, so that was reason enough in itself to be there. I saw Alice was getting her finger and toenails done so I asked for the same. Rose, the hand and foot lady, moved in and simultaneously soaked, cleaned, scraped, sharpened, buffed and painted every outcrop of claw tissue I possessed. She followed me to the washbasin and continued, remarking that I must have been very pretty when I was young. I decided not to punish her for this remark as she was at that moment trying to penetrate my soft tissue with a small pickaxe. Alice got gold polish and I got red. In Vietnam you can easily live like a queen: my shampoo, blow-dry and nail job cost US$10. And there was no diddling Alice — she questioned every bill, told people exactly what she thought and was generous with those who were kind.

Alice and I ate together at various restaurants, some luxurious and some hilariously downmarket. At the gorgeous Hoi An restaurant with its traditional antique wooden architecture, we ate salt and pepper soft shell crab. I thought this was a Chinese dish but Alice said no, it was the French who taught the Vietnamese to cook with pepper and salt. Before the French, the Vietnamese didn't have salt and used nuoc mam to add pungency to dishes. They taught it to (those bloody) Chinese and now the crafty bastards are taking credit for it. Soft shell is the only way to eat crab, and it's the cheat's way, because not only is it delicious but there's no carrying on and no mess. You simply eat the whole thing — claws, shell, inside, outside, because everything is soft. These crabs are quite expensive as you have to catch them while they're moulting, before the new shell hardens, and you've only got a window of an hour and a half. Can you imagine the drama? As we left the restaurant, a taxi driver bumped a man off his bicycle. Nobody took any notice.

Saigon is the capital of international food in Vietnam and a lot of the top-level hotel kitchens are run by foreigners, most of whom are young men. They are gastronomic gypsies, travelling the world from a young age, notching up incredible CVs, going where the good jobs are — London, Paris, New York, Hong Kong, Singapore. They not only have to be good chefs but also have to be able to run large brigades of mostly untrained or badly trained locals. Fortunately the Vietnamese are good cooks but, of course, there are language problems and cultural differences. I was walking by the posh five-star Caravelle Hotel and on the spur of the moment popped in to ask for my contact there, Brad Turley. The next thing I knew I was in the huge, spotless kitchen of Asian Reflections, their signature restaurant, drinking a glass of soda and watching head chef Brad put together his version of fish chowder. The saffron-suffused soup was dark burnt orange and deconstructed with the individual shellfish sitting in their shells. These were topped off with a prawn cracker filled with prawn aioli.

We sat down at the bar as I devoured a dish he had prepared, to give me an idea of his style. It was okra stuffed with shrimp, coriander and garlic and deep-fried in tempura batter, accompanied by a tiger prawn, some Vietnamese goat cheese and a salad of tiny leaves. I ate lots of Brad's food and it was all good but this first dish, for me, encapsulated all that is meritorious in mixing great cuisines. We don't use the dirty word fusion any more so I'll call it French method with strong Vietnamese overtones – French finger work with Asian ingredients. It was light, delectable and faultless.

Most of the top non-Vietnamese chefs in Saigon are Australian and Brad seems to be the only American. He is tall, blond, good looking and a very nice, open person, willing to talk about the thing he loves most – food. Although from San Francisco, he really learned his trade in Hawaii for five years with noted chef Roy Yamaguchi, then found himself working in New York for three years. He's been at the beautiful Asian Reflections for eight months and describes his cooking as South East Asian.

'What I love about Vietnamese food is the simple but clear flavours and the huge variety of seafood, fish and herbs. There are herbs I haven't even put my finger on yet. What I want to do is find out how Vietnamese really cook at home then add my own interpretation. My personal favourite so far is barbecued goat's nipples. In terms of my career I still consider myself a learner.'

Brad finds his Vietnamese staff very eager to learn but quite conservative. 'They have to be encouraged to intensify flavours – they'll always be careful rather than adventurous. They actually have no concept whatsoever of the Western palate which is why, when you go to French and Italian restaurants with Vietnamese chefs, the food always tastes Asian. They can't help themselves. The chefs here not only learn from me, I've learnt a lot from them, mainly patience and calmness. If you lose your cool with Vietnamese they just freeze and can't do anything. The French method of abuse and screaming in the kitchen would have everyone jumping out of the windows here.'

Brad's huge menu is like Donald's at the Press Club in Hanoi in that you can taste the food as soon as you look at the list. It's a very eclectic menu of contrasting textures and tastes and his personal specials are all Vietnamese/Japanese/Western fusions, like turmeric mashed potatoes, coconut-encrusted lamb rack with stir-fried curry noodles, seared sea bass with miso carrot mash and peppercorn tamarind bonito broth. Then there are classic sexy Italian dishes using mozzarella; marscapone tortellini with walnut parmesan cream; garlic seared octopus and shrimp with chorizo, tomato and corn risotto. His American side comes out with the nostalgic barbecued pork cutlet with dried apple country hash and minted strawberry pepper sauce! And his boy side explodes with no less than ten steak dishes using imported American grain-fed beef. The wine list is outrageous, crawling with French premiere crus and even a Smith Haut Lafitte, for heaven's sake. When Americans are in town, they come straight to Brad and if, as sometimes happens, they order a well-done steak with fries and say they'd like to meet the chef, Brad hides under the kitchen bench.

He gets a lot of his vegetables, fruit and European supplies from 'Veggy's' (trademark name Golden Garden), a flash grocery owned and run by American Bob Allen and his Vietnamese wife Nguyen Thi Hue. Veggy's is a tiny shop on Le Thanh Ton Street in a groovy little upmarket area of coffee shops (these are real coffee shops, not cafés, where they sell top-quality coffee beans), hair salons, Japanese restaurants, expensive children's clothing shops and interior design houses. Bob's shop has garlic hanging outside and wooden bins overflowing with vegetables. You step in and meet with a world of imported canned, bottled and boxed European products which have nothing to do with Vietnam. I can see a swagger of homesick ex-pats salivating over Marmite, sesame crackers, jams and La Vache Qui Rit processed cheese. Actually La Vache Qui Rit, brought over by the French, is now completely Vietnamese. It is so processed that it can sit in the heat all day on some godforsaken country stall with no fridge and still be edible. You just put a few of the triangular segments in a baguette and voilà, happiness.

The *best* part of the shop is through the glass-panelled door that leads to the inner sanctum, the heart of longing, the secret closet – the cold room. This crowded little room with groaning shelves of produce is also a great place to be on a hot day, so I took my time perusing it. I inhaled ricotta, Australian chèvre, buffalo mozzarella, blue cheeses, cream, butter, feta, brie, brick and camembert. I tried not to touch the cherry tomatoes, bunches of Italian basil and thyme and tarragon, asparagus, mixed greens, Avignon radishes, French beans, button mushrooms and baby red capsicums. There were passion-fruit, raspberries, kiwifruit, strawberries, honey dew melons, avocados and edible flowers. One whole corner was devoted to charcuterie like jambon cru, salami, ham, bacon and sausages.

And then I met Bob and his wife, who are uncommonly nice people. He explained to me that, in consultation with the Horticulture and Food Research Institute of New Zealand, they started a 'clean green' programme of growing their produce in Da Lat and that they are as close to organic as is possible. No sprays are used and the ground is fertilised with fish emulsion and mulched. This tiny shop belies the huge size of the business. Their principal market is wholesaling to restaurants and hotels, both in Vietnam and Cambodia. Bob told me that France is providing the biggest trade and financial input at present in Vietnam and the French food supplier METRO have recently moved in. Bob didn't tell me this but I know that doing business with the Vietnamese is always a risk. They love getting foreigners to help them set up businesses by investing money and know-how, then rip them off and dump them.

After four days I left the house of Alice's cousin and stayed at two different hotels in Saigon, the Rex and the Continental. Alice knew the owner of the Rex dans le temps – in the old days. 'The owner was related to the imperial family which is why the hotel was called Rex. When Saigon fell in 1975, the Rex was taken over by the Communists and, to humiliate him, they forced my friend to be the doorman and live in a little cubby-hole next to the doors for eight years. His wife had previously escaped to Paris and was living in a big apartment. She couldn't come back and he couldn't get out. Finally she arranged for him to leave Vietnam.

He's still alive but she went mad and died. And now there's the Communist flag flying over that wonderful hotel.'

The gaudy Rex was the hotel of my dreams, the best sort of place to stay in a city with a murky past. The decor is absolutely, thrillingly 1930s matured kitsch/tropical Vietnamese and it has everything: beautiful ornate restaurants, the best rooftop bar in Saigon madly decorated with caged birds, cane furniture and potted bonsais shaped like animals, a bank, a business centre, a tailor, acupuncture, a swimming pool, a gym and, right at the very top overlooking the whole city, a caged tennis court! My lovely room was right next to the terrace but at the quiet end and beneath the swimming pool. It had old-fashioned furniture, little puff stools for sitting on while you powdered your nose at the mirror, a satin bedspread, an outrageous tacky lampshade atop a classic porcelain vase and a charming bathroom. I was in heaven.

I had the obligatory B52 cocktail on the roof amid sparkling lights and elephant sculptures and breakfast in the golden restaurant with lemon satin cushions on the chairs. This was the breakfast to beat all breakfasts, an international feast, including half a dozen fresh fruit juices, that stretched along two full walls of the large room – and it was all part of the price. The staff were adorable and very helpful in explaining why you should eat what looked like glue with shrimps in it, miniature white pancakes and soup for breakfast. But if you didn't want to go Vietnamese, hey, the world was your oyster. I watched what could only have been a rugby player get up six times to try different breakfasts. How I deduced he was a rugby player was by the damaged face, the cabbage ears, the scratching of the groin and the neanderthal gait. Have you ever watched a rugby player eat? It's like watching a child who has been brought up by wolves. I'm sure his mother loves him.

Then, because I had pre-booked the Continental at a good price through a contact and didn't feel I could get out of it, I was unfortunately obliged to decamp. I had chosen this hotel from home as a result of romantic illusions incurred after reading Graham Greene's brilliant novel *The Quiet American*, which was written there. When I told Alice I was staying at the Continental, she informed me the owner Philippe Franchini was another friend who had had his hotel confiscated by Uncle Ho and was now a well-known painter and writer in Paris. He has written a very moving book of memoirs called *Continental Saigon*. The hotel, built in 1922, has recently had US$4 million spent on air-conditioning, new lifts, restoring the wide hallways and lobbies to their original decoration and design, painting the exterior in white and ivory and installing new furniture. My room was huge but depressing and could have been splendid if someone had had a jot of taste. There was no pretty decor, brown and green 1960s tiles in the bathroom and no natural light. The curtains had to remain closed because I looked straight into the bar and it into me. I missed the eccentric decoration of the Rex and my swimming pool room terribly.

Finally I couldn't bear being shut in any longer and asked for another room with a view. This was still fairly egalitarian but had a sort of day room with heavy Chinese furniture and windows opening onto the street. The courtyard with outside tables was quite pretty but the dining room was like eating in a Russian canteen. Breakfast was a tawdry joke (these people need to take a walk around the corner to the Rex to see how it's done) with mugs rather than cups for lukewarm tea, one choice of juice, pathetic single-egg omelettes and pho made with macaroni one morning because they had run out of noodles! Running out of noodles in Vietnam is like running out of words in a library – a physical impossibility.

And yet the Continental was desperately fashionable in its heyday. Anyone who didn't have a jot of work to do and possessed a good wardrobe in creased linen, lay around the terrace smoking Gauloises and drinking apéritifs, sharing secrets, scandals and speculations, swapping incredible stories and heroic tales and indulging in sordid proposals. Killing the Cochinois boredom of life in the tropics, high society women draped themselves in long robes and came to take tea on Thursday and Sunday afternoons, and on Saturdays one danced on the outside stage in front of the municipal theatre across the road. The Continental is on Dong Khoi Street (General Insurrection Street), renamed unglamorously but staunchly by the Communists, in the centre of downtown Saigon. Called Rue Catinat in the time of the French, it was infamous for its carryings-on. The 1950s was a great time to be on Rue Catinat when Europeans, both French and American, listened to jazz and drank whisky, kir and vermouth-cassis and played quatre cent vingt-et-un dice games. There were private clubs from which Chinese and Vietnamese were excluded, there was opium trading and gossiping about who was bribing whom, who was having an affair with whom and how ghastly the oppressive heat was, chère. During difficulties between the French and the Communists, restaurants and cafés had grilles on the windows to prevent bullets or bombs flying in. It didn't always work and if someone got shot, the waiters just cleaned up the mess, wiped the blood off the walls and carried on serving the entrecote Béarnaise.

One thing at the Continental of which I wholly approved was the massage service. In my experience, the best massages to be had in Vietnam are in good hotels. The back street ones are exciting and give you a look into Vietnamese shadows but they are pretty brutal and repetitive. The masseuses at hotels are trained and have a greater repertoire. At the Continental, I put my clothes into a locker, was given a bottle of water, showered and lay down in an air-conditioned room. The white uniformed girl sat on top of me and massaged my body with her body using her feet and arms and thighs, then walked on my back and legs steadying herself by holding onto a bar on the ceiling. Her movements were considered and she had been taught correctly. How guys stay sane during this I can't imagine but the 'rules' clearly state that the massages are straight and no prostitutes are allowed in the hotel (or toxics or explosives or pets for that matter, because I checked). When I asked male friends if they got aroused during these massages, they came over all coy.

One of the great gastronomic pleasures in international Saigon is the Japanese restaurants. They're relatively expensive if you're a true gastronome but the fish is so violently fresh, it makes you weep. I'm a sushi freak, and nowhere in the world have I eaten such fresh sushi. It's not a day old, it's hours old, sometimes minutes old, and so tender and fragrant you can't believe it. The only thing I could compare it with is catching fish off the back of a launch and eating it with soy sauce and wasabi (Japanese green horseradish) right there and then. There's something sweet about truly fresh seafood too — if you eat scallops raw, they taste quite different from cooked. Speaking of wasabi, in my favourite Japanese restaurant in Saigon, K Café on Hai Ba Trung Street near the Continental, they served fresh wasabi with the food. I was sitting at the bar scanning as usual and my eye fell on the familiar knobbly rhizome sitting on the counter. I thought I was imagining things. Nobody serves fresh wasabi because it's so perishable, expensive and elusive. Once grated from the root, it loses its heat very quickly and there it was, in front of me with my name written on it. The customers took it when they felt the urge and grated some onto their plates with the fine bamboo grater provided. The Japanese gentleman sitting next to me told me it was grown in Da Lat and we fell into conversation.

He told me he was a seafood dealer — buying shrimp in Vietnam and selling it to Japan — and I told him I was a travel/food writer. The waitresses at K Café were very wenchy and cheeky in their black mini-skirts and tight black T-shirts with the big white 'K' on the front. At first they had that uninterested, blank look on their faces but quite quickly they became adorable and doting. They had put me right next to their service area at the bar so they leaned over and on me to do their bills. I liked such familiarity because I got all sorts of information out of them. They petted me and stroked me and made comments on my hair: was it natural, where did I get my clothes, what was I writing and where was my husband? This atmosphere was obviously tolerated and encouraged by the boss Jimmy, resplendent in candy pink shirt and expansive demeanour. He and Mr Japan pointed to a pomegranate on the bench and asked me what it was called in English. I had to tell them over and over again because they couldn't believe a word could be so long.

'But what does it mean?' they asked.

'Pomme is French for apple and granate is from the Latin granatum meaning full of seeds.'

'Ohhhhhhh,' everyone said in unison.

I was thrilled that such a simple explanation had given me an air of unexpected credibility.

Mr Japan had a conversation about me in English with the Vietnamese waitress and because neither of them was speaking their native tongue, they seemed to assume I couldn't hear or understand.

'I think I'll ask her out but she doesn't seem very enthusiastic.'

'She cold. She Western. She can't help it.'

'I think I'll ask her anyway.'

To me he said, 'Shall we meet?'

'No,' I replied.

'No?'

'No.'

'But it's just to discuss business and food.'

'Where is your wife tonight?'

'She doesn't understand me (surprise, surprise). She is Vietnamese and tries to control me.'

But he wasn't all heartless. He had ordered some cheap sushi roll to take home for his wife while he himself ate the most expensive things he could think of, including lots of Japanese saki.

The next day I was enjoying the traffic noise and fanning myself on a street corner, having bought some ruffled silk garments from Song dress shop.

'I've seen you before,' said a girl's voice.

I looked around then looked down. 'I'm sure you have. The whole of Vietnam has seen me by now.'

'No I have. I know you need some of my postcards.'

The girl smiling up at me spoke such flawless conversational American-accented English that I stared at her. She had an intelligent and sassy face, short pixie-cut hair and a demeanour much older than her age, which appeared to be about 10.

'Stop with the postcards already. Okay, let me think. Oh, I know. What I really want is a version of Marguerite Duras's novel *The Lover* in English or French, preferably English.'

An almost imperceptible movement from her and a short, staccato popping of orders prompted a masked woman on a honda to do an about turn and speed off.

'*The Lover* will be here in a minute.'

'Who was that?'

'My mother. She has gone to get it for you.'

Now that's what I call service. While I was waiting, a European man came up and had a conversation with her, asking her how she was and what she was up to. 'He was my English teacher at school,' she explained to me.

The mother zoomed back not only with my book but also with *The North China Lover* by Duras. The girl charged a whopping price for the photocopied books (all books are cheap, illegal copies in Vietnam and most of the print is crooked on the page) but I didn't care. I wanted them and I wanted her.

'Come and have a coffee with me,' I said.

'Okay.'

Her name is Tran Thu Ha, called Ha and she controls Saigon. She's 14 years old and runs the joint, pays for nothing, is a one-girl tourist bureau, supports her entire family and is seriously brainy. Ha is very tiny, probably suffering from either a growth condition or malnutrition, and looks like a mini-woman, not a child. She's not one of those dumb, pretty Saigon chicks with ponytails and short skirts who use their charm and looks to get sales. She wears jeans, flip-flops, a velvet top and a sensible hat, but allows her feminine side to express itself in a line-up of six rings in her ear and blue and red hair extensions attached by combs. She would accept only a glass of water, no matter how much ice cream or cake I offered her. She sat confidently at a window table at Givraly Café across the road from the Continental and told me her story. Since the age of four, when her father died, Ha has been selling postcards and books on the street to support her family. Her aunts are in on it too and mother is always close by on the honda but don't think for one second the mother is in charge. Ha goes to school from 6 a.m. till 8.30 a.m. then crosses the Saigon River from the other side where she lives, and works the central area between the Continental and the Rex till 7 p.m. Her favourite foods are chicken or fish with rice, hamburgers and hotdogs. She has three younger brothers who enjoy a normal full day at school thanks to her income.

'I suppose when you get home in the evening, your brothers cook you dinner and rub your feet?'

'Are you kidding?' she smiled ruefully. 'Boys do nothing and they get everything.'

'Would you marry a Vietnamese boy?'

'I don't think so. I would prefer to marry a foreigner like an Australian or an American, someone who has more respect for women.'

'What is your best subject at school?'

'Math and history.'

'Any languages?'

'I speak a bit of French, Japanese and Chinese.'

'What do you like most about your job?'

'Tour guiding because I get to go all over the place. It stops me from being bored.'

'Your pet hate?'

'Rude people who tell me to go away without even looking at me. What do they mean, go away? It's my country.'

'In an ideal world, what would you like to do with your life apart from run Saigon?'

'I don't run Saigon! I want to go to university and become a lawyer.'

If Ha does not grow up to become president of Vietnam or run a mega successful business in the States, something will have gone terribly wrong. Her mobile rang, she barked some orders into it, probably telling her aunts to get the pot boiling for dinner, looked around and I could see she was restless. Ha is so intelligent and loaded with personality, she can't stand being idle – no time for it.

'What do you want to do, Peta?'

'Let's go to the market.'

She raced off down the road, walking straight through old women squatting over their braziers, napalmed cripples begging and tourists slouching.

'Ha, I can't keep up with you.'

'Oh sorry. I've learnt to walk slowly for tourists. This is me walking slowly.'

She taught me how to cross the road. I knew that the best way to cross eight lanes of insane Saigon traffic was to walk slowly but confidently, giving motorists time to avoid you. If you do it fast, they're more likely to hit you. Nevertheless I was wary and always kept a close eye on the traffic, often standing back for a honda or car as I wound my way across. Ha just steps out and walks across without making eye contact with anyone. She's the size of a clothes peg so this made me very nervous.

'Peta,' she said, exasperated, 'you are in charge. You must be more confident, like this.' She grabbed my hand and dragged me screaming across the road. 'You look straight ahead with your shoulders back and you don't give an inch.'

'I'm going to die.'

'Don't be dramatic.' Eyes raised to heaven.

We stopped to look in shop windows and I could see her mouthing a conversation to someone across the road.

'Who are you talking to?'

'My mother.'

'Tell her to come with us.'

'Oh no. She would get bored.'

The whole family suffers from boredom. If they're not working and slaving all day, they get bored. She took my bags, looked at my hands severely and said, 'Peta, take those rings and bracelets off. You've got too much jewellery on. There are lots of people in Saigon who would cut your fingers off for those rings if they got you alone.'

Banh Mi
Vietnamese Baguette

Makes 2 loaves of bread

120 g (1 cup) of rice flour

140 g (1 cup) white wheat flour

2 tsp dry yeast

1 tbsp sugar

1 cup warm water

2 tbsp melted butter

1 tsp salt

1 Sift together the rice flour, wheat flour and salt.
2 Place the yeast, sugar and a cup of warm water in a mixer, fitted with the dough blade or hook. Get the mixer going at its slowest speed, add the butter then gradually add the dry ingredients. Increase the speed and keep going for another couple of minutes till you have a smooth dough.
3 Place the dough in a greased bowl, cover with a damp tea towel or plastic wrap and leave in a warm place for about an hour or until it has doubled in volume. The dough is quite wet for a bread dough – this is normal.
4 Turn out onto a floured bench and knead for 1 minute. Divide in 2 and shape into 2 baguettes about 18 cm (7 in) long. Place on a floured cookie tray, cover and leave again for an hour to double in size.
5 Pre-heat the oven to 200°C (400°F). With a razor blade or very sharp knife, make 3 diagonal slits across the top of the loaves. Place in the oven and bake about 20 minutes till golden. The outside should be crisp.

We entered the vast covered Ben Thanh market and everybody knew her. She got a lot of razzing about the new hair colours and where she'd been for so long and how come she never visited any more.

'This used to be one of my runs – that's why they all know me. See all these clothes stalls around the outside of the market? Exactly the same stuff is inside but it costs half the price. This costs more because it's government controlled and it's a scam.'

This market is clean and ordered with stalls arranged in an aesthetic Français sort of way. It's probably a bit more expensive than an outdoor market but lots of tourists come here so it's less anarchic. We bought a kilo of top-quality Vietnamese Arabica coffee and wound our way down through a narrow aisle reeking with dried and pickled fish in orange mountains, dried bamboo hearts and tangerine rice paper to find some nuoc mam sauce. Ha grabbed a bottle.

'No, no, not that one. It has to be from Phu Quoc Island,' I said.

'Why?'

'Because it's the best.'

'Oh', she yelped, slapping her forehead, 'you're an expert in fish sauce now.'

'I will be. Watch this space,' I replied, opening my mouth and pointing to it.

I really wanted to get to Phu Quoc Island, with its primeval forests and golden beaches, to visit the fish sauce factory, but because the heat and humidity ensure more senior moments than usual, I missed the plane. The little aircraft to Phu Quoc goes three times a week and by the time I'd pulled my synapses together, all flights were booked out for the next two weeks, so I just had to imagine the ecstasy of being in a room full of decomposing, secreting fish. Phu Quoc is a very beautiful little island off the coast of southern Vietnam, perilously close to Cambodia; in fact the Cambodians think they own it but the Vietnamese are quite sure they don't, which accounts for the large military presence there. Using a chemical process to turn a primary product into something else which enhances the world's range of food sources is a truly magical process. It's like coffee, olives, cheese and wine. No one would touch raw coffee beans or olives and who would have thought, as they crouched in their rank cave ruining their teeth on a knuckle of baby dinosaur, that milk could be turned into solid cheese by a process of controlled rotting, and grapes turned into liquid gold by a bit of yeast?

Whether you like the taste of fish sauce or not depends entirely on your own sensibilities. Some people describe the smell as like tiger's urine, rotten seaweed, strongly sexual, as if someone hadn't washed for a few days, disgusting. Those who love it, like me, find it intensely tangy, pungent but delicate and completely, fishily delicious. Whatever you think, the fact is that nuoc mam is good for you, full of amino acids, nitrogen, sodium chloride, phosphorus, calcium and fluoride. Until you've tasted Vietnamese nuoc mam you would never think there could be another use for the liquid of decomposing fish. Well, humans have consumed worse. When I was on the island of Ischia in southern Italy, I visited the dungeon of a medieval convent and viewed the commode-like seats on which dead nuns were placed, to sit and rot. As a form of barbaric meditation on how they were going to end up, postulants were forced to spend weeks alone with these holy corpses and as the flesh decomposed and fermented, they supped on the juices therein. Some went mad, some starved to death and others lost their sense of humour.

For centuries, different cultures have fermented fish into sauces. The Greeks and Romans did it to make garum and liquamen, the Scandinavians do it to herrings with salt, sugar and spices, the Italians and Spanish do it to anchovies, the Africans do it to large fish, the Tahitians use sea water to do it, the English use it as the basis of Gentleman's Relish and Worcestershire sauce and the Asians use it in the most sophisticated ways of all. Vietnamese fish sauce is different from all other Asian fish sauces, with its own distinctive flavour and clarity, and to my mind, it's the best. Phu Quoc nuoc mam is made from tiny, translucent, anchovy-like fish called ca com, which are layered with at least 20 per cent of sea salt in huge, round wooden barrels like open wine casks held together with thick rope. They obtain the salt by boiling sea water over a rice-husk fire and scooping off the salt as it crystallises on the surface. The fish sit in the barrels in the heat for three months till the stench is just about unbearable, then the resultant liquid is drained off from a tap at the bottom. It's poured straight back into the barrel and you walk away for another three months. The liquid is again drained off, strained and bottled. This first extraction liquid, which is quite dark and very thick, is called ngon or thuong hang. It's the crème de la crème, the grand cru, the je ne sais quoi of fish sauces. And guess what? Just like a fine wine, top-quality nuoc mam improves in the bottle with age. Connoisseurs 'put down' superior bottles in the cellar till they peak.

At this point, they start producing second and third grades of sauce by topping up the mash in the barrels with water, draining, filtering and bottling. These bottles, mainly used for cooking rather than sprinkling, are left in the sun for a few days till the colour intensifies into a light caramel. So why doesn't the fish keep rotting and poison us? Because at 20 per cent salt, the fermentation micro-organisms will stop multiplying at a certain point, which leads to autolysis. I have to say the real thing is very strong and most people prefer it calmed down by adding lime juice, sugar, water, chilli and garlic to make nuoc cham. Phu Quoc fish sauce is so good that Unilever of Great Britain and the Phu Quoc Fish Sauce Producers' Association have reached an agreement to build a swish new bottling plant on the island, with the kind contribution of $US10 million from Unilever.

Judging by her size, Ha is not interested in food so we were out of the market again and down the road to a cheap Internet place she knew of. Internet prices at the Continental were twice the price of anywhere else so I was grateful for the information. Foreigners she knows stopped to talk to her on the street all the time; it was like trying to take a stroll with a movie star. Sometimes they stopped to talk to me if they knew me from my television food show. Ha was impressed – two famous people trying to walk down the road together. She spent as long as she liked on the Internet and didn't pay a cent, gave me her e-mail address and mobile number, brought me cold Cokes. Vietnamese either don't charge each other for Internet access or charge very low prices and concentrate on fleecing the visitors. They especially like fleecing the Japanese, who are always loaded. Europeans are the next most desirable hit because they're gullible and their Protestant guilt gets in the way of the haggling process.

As we were walking down the street, a gaggle of giggling Chinese girls asked me to photograph them.

'They wouldn't ask me,' said Ha, 'they think I would steal their camera.'

'But their bags are lying there under a tree for anyone to steal.'

'There's nothing in them. Anyone who knows anything, knows that. No one would bother to steal from a Chinese.'

I ran into Ha every so often after that and we always went for a walk or had a drink together. She symbolised Saigon people for me – tough, knowledgeable, lovable and funny.

I had been advised to make my visits to Can Tho in the Mekong Delta and Da Lat in the central highlands from the base of Saigon, rather than just keep wandering around with a huge suitcase full of Vietnamese cooking utensils, 300 different coloured Chinese flip-flops and heavy but indispensable cookbooks. Not to mention the hand luggage bag, laptop, conical hat and Mandarina Duck shoulder bag. I left almost everything at the hotel and set off for Can Tho with only what would fit in the hand luggage bag. It felt good to be so light.

6

Can Tho

When you pronounce Can Tho the way it looks, no one in Vietnam understands you. The correct pronunciation of 'o' is hard for a Westerner to get their tongue around. It's sort of like a long 'er' but not really. 'Th' is 't' so Can Tho is Can-ter. I hired Alice's driver Canh for three days and two nights for the sum of US$100. For that price he did the return trip from Saigon to Can Tho in the Mekong Delta, drove anywhere else I wanted, disappeared into thin air when I didn't need him and as he didn't speak one single word of English or French and I not one of Vietnamese, we mostly existed in blissful silence. He gave me green tiger balm to cool my temples and when he wanted to communicate, he phoned his friend who spoke English and put her on the line.

'Canh want know if you hungry.'

'Yes,' I would reply.

'Canh want know what you want eat.'

'Pho.'

'Okay. Pho.'

We negotiated the insane traffic out of Saigon in his little car and he inevitably ran into a cyclist, tipped him off, jumped out, put him back on again, apologised and kept driving. I was in the back seat suffering from shock and thinking, I've got four more hours of this. On the highway south we passed bikes and hondas and cyclos carrying anything and everything – giant funeral flower arrangements, cows, entire families, beds, hay, food both live and cooked, crates of beer. The roadsides were littered with vehicles that had played chicken and lost. We passed a crowd of people watching with interest as a truck was hauled out of someone's front yard by another truck. No question of police or insurance or witnesses. Later on, we encountered two tailgating trucks that had run into each other. The highway was littered with glass and shocked people sat on the road. Head injuries resulting from traffic accidents are the number one cause of accidental deaths in Saigon. My editor found this statement in the newspaper: 'Soaring traffic accidents caused by poor driving, bad roads and a rapid increase in the number of motor bikes killed 9584 people and injured 23,981 others in Vietnam in the first nine months of this year (2002). Last year 10,624 people were killed on the roads and last month, which Vietnam observed as traffic safety month, 980 people were killed.'

I was going to Can Tho because it's the bread basket of Vietnam – they can grow absolutely anything there. It is also the home of the best rice paper and rice noodle making and a horror restaurant. Five gruelling hours later we found ourselves at the ferry that would take us across the river to Can Tho. In Vietnam they'll sell you anything under any conditions, so running alongside the car as it edged forward in the tiresome ferry queue were people bearing plates of huge pies, head trays loaded with sugar cane to suck on, banh bao (rice buns), peeled pomelo, baguettes, Coke, sunglasses, beer, tiny orange roasted birds (or mice), packets of rice paper. What are you going to do with rice paper in the car – roll it around a piece of chocolate or maybe make a fan out of it? And everyone was so good-natured and enjoying their little lives, no matter how hard, and having a great laugh at my hair and freckles. But I have to be frank here – they're in no position to laugh. The peasant women have got to get over the endemic wearing of pyjamas. Yes, pyjamas, real Western pyjamas. I know they're practical but it's not a good look, especially when their normal clothes are so pretty and cheap, and the girls are so beautiful. Here's the ensemble: pyjamas, another mismatching shirt over the top, face mask, conical hat. Why doesn't someone tell them they're wearing pyjamas? As Joan Rivers said when Stevie Wonder had beaded dreadlocks in the 1980s, why doesn't someone tell him he's wearing a macramé plant holder on his head?

The tropical Mekong Delta is fertile, lush and green, and it produces enough rice to feed the whole nation, with lots left over. It exports the most rice in the world after Thailand. We drove into downtown Can Tho, which is a bit of a dump really, rejected the first hotel as too depressing and I found myself at the new Golf Hotel in a prime location right on the Can Tho River. Gulf Hotel is a mausoleum of money, sufficient shiny bad taste to give you a headache and not enough customers. The only other guests seemed to be Korean businessmen who hung out in the 'friendship' bar, got dodgy Thai massages on the first floor and made a lot of noise in the karaoke Babylon on the river. Is there anything less sexy in the whole world than a travelling, low-level businessman? The hotel was inundated with R&R spaces: the tenth floor had a brand-new French restaurant with a French chef and zero customers, the eighth floor had another outdoor restaurant, the second a coffee shop, the first a swimming pool and massage room, the ground a restaurant and bar, and the basement the friendship bar. What is it with Asian businessmen? Do they require a huge social life? Hong Kong I can understand, but the middle of the Mekong Delta? Anyway for US$60 a night and a room on the river, I had only to incline my head an inch and the whole hotel would come running, so who was I to complain, n'est-ce pas?

The first thing I did after plugging in my laptop and checking my e-mails was hit Hai Ba Trung Street on the riverfront, to see what was what in the throbbing metropolis of Can Tho. There amid the busyness is the smallest, most beautiful Chinese pagoda I have ever seen. The Ong Temple is dedicated to the worship of Quan Am Buddha and reminded me of the heavily ornate old churches in Southern France and Italy, where they have everything from model ships to old photos to pay-your-way-to-heaven candles. Ushered into the temple by two porcelain unicorns, you enter a dark red and gold world, heavily sensual and languidly thick with dozens of giant conical coils of incense hung from the ceiling. There are ornamental tree vases, huge copper incense burners, bas-relief sculptures in gold, red candles burning and three alters with deities in fantastical gowns and headdress. In front of the Buddha were offerings of fruit and even a bottle of nuoc mam, which I found most thoughtful.

On the other side of the road from the pagoda is a giant silver statue of Ho Chi Minh which looks exactly like the tin man in *The Wizard of Oz*. Every time I walked past I expected to see Judy Garland popping her head around the side. Just past him starts a market so wonderful and picturesque that those who know better are planning to destroy it and replace it with a nice shopping mall. This would not only be really depressing but would wipe out an entire culture and lifestyle for the farmers and fishers of Hung Phu Island on the other side of the river. Every day, starting about 4 a.m., they cross over in their boats to deliver fabulous produce to the market: durian, mangosteen, oranges, tiny red crab-apples, little green apples they eat with ginger, grapes, yellow pomegranates, peaches striated exactly like apples, green guavas with pink flesh, pale green star fruit, papaya, limes, pineapple. People crouch on their haunches over baskets of tomatoes, cherry-sized eggplants, bright yellow pumpkins, long green okra, galangal, knobbly bitter melon, taro and fat, cooked corn on the cob. Everything is in perfect condition, screaming with colour and trimmed, sorted and presented like still lifes.

Can Tho central market is also famous for its shellfish, snakes and river fish. There are trays of huge snails, some of them going for a stroll, frogs, eels, catfish, squid, crabs — all shining and quivering. I don't know if the bras and knickers are grown on the island but they were there too, among the fish and pork paté. The women pinched my arms and smiled and pointed to my hair. Everyone crowded around to watch me writing in my notebook, asking for my bright pink fan and encouraging me to say hello to their babies. In the dim, covered part of the market I found my way to a food stall and sat down when invited. The quiet woman put a fresh spring roll in front of me with a spicy sauce. It was divine. Then she took her scissors and snipped half a dozen morsels of marinated grilled pork off a skewer onto a bowl of rice and waited for me to eat it – again divine.

Later on in the day I got all revved up for my 'superb' dinner at the 'best' restaurant in Can Tho. The guidebook waxed lyrical about the thoughtfully restored, classic French villa. What I found was a very tired restaurant, resting on whatever laurels it had once had, which served me up Western style food in spite of the fact that I ordered from the Vietnamese section. I ate three pieces of rigid, deep-fried, battered squid, threw the glass of Da Lat vang rouge down my gullet, pushed the rest away and ran back down into the street where I belong. The evenings are temperate in Can Tho so it's comfortable to walk around and a relief not to be pouring with sweat. Soon I found a little, wizened old woman squatting beside her pot full of mysteries. It was like pulling rabbits out of a hat. She smiled and held my hand and pulled out some hot somethings on skewers. These she squirted with two kinds of sauce, placed them carefully in a little box, pinched my arm and sent me on my way. I walked down to the river, sat on a bench, gave a free English lesson to some enthusiastic English language students and examined my feast. The little bits of marinated pork, wrapped in leaves and grilled, was delicious and sweet beyond endurance. I was in love. I just couldn't get over how lucky the Vietnamese were to be able to eat these fast food taste sensations any time they wanted for practically nothing. The trick is to eat small amounts whenever you feel like it, as the Vietnamese themselves do. That way you taste lots of things and never feel too full and, most importantly, never have to say no.

The Can Tho tourist office is hilarious – peeling pink walls and everyone dressed in blue shirts and madly enthusiastic. If you wish to use their services you have to specify your touristic desires clearly to the entire office staff, who possess varying aptitudes at English, fill in and sign a form elucidating your specific desires and pay for them there and then in advance. The whole office nods and smiles approvingly and you back out,

Goi Cuon
Fresh Spring Rolls

Vietnamese rice paper is very fine so it just needs to be wiped with a damp cloth and it is soft and ready to be eaten. However, most rice paper you buy will have to be soaked for a few minutes. I prefer to have all the ingredients ready on the table and let guests make their own, but if you make them in advance, do so as close to eating time as possible and cover with a damp towel or plastic wrap.

Serves 4 to 6

120 g (4 oz) dried rice vermicelli
120 g (4 oz) pork belly or loin
18 medium-sized prawns or shrimp, shelled
12 round rice papers 15 to 20 cm (6 to 8 in) in diameter
about 12 lettuce leaves
150 g (1 cup) finely julienned carrot
lots of fresh mint, Vietnamese mint (tangier) or coriander leaves
nuoc leo or nuoc cham dipping sauce

1   Soak the vermicelli in warm water till soft – about 15 minutes.
2   Bring a pot of water to the boil and place the vermicelli in a sieve. Lower it into the boiling water for 15 seconds, then rinse immediately in cold water. Put aside, covered in plastic wrap.
3   Add some salt and in the same water cook the pork for 10 minutes. Remove, rinse in cold water and slice thinly.
4   In the same water, cook the prawns for 1 minute. Rinse in cold water, cut in half lengthwise and devein.
5   Soak 4 rice papers at a time in warm water for a few minutes till they become opaque and soft. Place on a tea towel.
6   On the bottom third of the rice paper (leave 2.5 cm (1 in) free on either side) place a piece of lettuce, about a tablespoon of vermicelli, some julienned carrot, 3 prawn halves, 3 pork slices and some mint or coriander leaves. Fold the wrapper once over the filling, fold in the sides, then roll up to the end. Some people leave the prawns and herbs to the last roll so they show through the paper. Also, you can leave one end open with the herbs and carrot sticking out. Cover with a damp tea towel or plastic wrap and make up the rest.

To serve: Pour sauce into individual little bowls and dip the rolls in.

doing the same thing. They gave me a conical hat with a pretty chin band, attached on either side by bows. I held it up to the light and poems in Chinese figures became visible. At precisely 6.55 a.m. the following day I reported for duty to the residing tourist officer, Duc, and was taken in a motorised long boat up the river to Cai Rang, the biggest floating market in the delta. When I made my booking this young man was very straight and humourless. Freedom from the office brought about an exceptional personality change in Duc. He waxed lyrical, flirted, sang old-fashioned American songs to me and generally took it easy. By the end of the trip, for which I was short-changed by half an hour, he was lying down on the seat with his feet up, seeing to his pimples and suggesting how I could waste even more money at the tourist office.

In spite of him the large, wholesale, floating market was stunning and very interesting. The delta is a huge system of thousands of rivers and canals covering several countries, so large it has two daily tides. The boat people have no fixed abode – they go where business is and the action starts before dawn. By the time we got there at 7.30 the market was in full swing, the sun already beating down and money changing hands like playing cards. Folk in small boats were gossiping and buying up large from the bigger boats, deftly manipulating their way in and around on the big river. The heavy scales were out and great loads of papaya, potatoes, yams, bananas, greens, herbs, pigs, fish and rice were being sold. There are floating mini-bars, supermarkets, restaurants – in fact a whole village. It's not loud or demanding and the floating lends it a dreamlike quality. I asked the driver to pull up alongside a floating kitchen, so he roped the boat to a bigger one, signalled the little kitchen boat and she hooked herself onto us. My breakfast was a sort of pho called bun, which is basically rice noodles in stock, and what's in it depends on where you are in the country. This bun had sliced banana flower, tomatoes, pork, sausage, crunchy bean sprouts and a plop of black squid ink paste. The kitchen lady handed the bowl through her window, stayed hooked on till I had finished, then took back her bowl and utensils and moved off.

We motored back along the river towards Hung Thanh village on

Tung Phu Island, a sort of tropical zoo garden with little homestays dotted around the property. It was very pretty with all the local spices and fruit growing and outdoor tables where you could eat. We were served tea and fruit. Two little monkeys had danced around each other's neck chains so often, they had got themselves very tightly entangled at the neck. One of them was choking, its eyes bulging; the other was beating it and nobody took any notice. I stood next to them and insisted somebody release the chain, which they eventually did but only because I made a fuss. Also dotted around the property were caged monkeys, alligators, geese, chickens, fruit bats, huge porcupines, pigeons, cats, eels, fish and snakes. I didn't feel right about this place but couldn't put my finger on it. The staff were very nice and relaxed and I kept staring at them to find an answer. A monkey in a wooden cage hanging from a tree was anxiously moving from one side to the other. Every time I approached, it lowered its depressed eyes in a most disturbing reflex. And why would a cat be in a cage? Why would a dozen bats be in a cage so small they could barely hang upside-down properly?

All life in the delta is related to the river. People wash themselves, their dishes and their clothes in it and dump all their garbage into it. Needless to say, this is now starting to cause pollution problems. The downside of living on a flood plain jungle paradise on a huge river is that when it rains, it really rains and the riverbank villages are flooded every year without fail. I was interested to see the houses built right at the water's edge, practically slipping into the river and not even on stilts – the water was literally sloshing into the dining room. Now, as sure as the sun shines, the river will flood every year. The people know this, they have known it for hundreds of years, so why do they build so close to the ground? Now there's a new government initiative to build houses on flood-free areas in the Mekong Delta. A household is provided with an interest-free loan of VN10 million to buy some of this land and a VND7 million loan at 3 per cent to buy building materials. All in all the government is planning to spend VND7 trillion on a four-year plan to keep people's ankles dry.

I went back to the woman in the market several times and her friends would come and watch me eat. They exchanged remarks like little birds, which I assume meant things like 'she'll eat anything this one … look at her … give her some of this … and this … maybe she's thirsty … give her some coconut water and see what happens.' They watched closely, got the nod from me and imperceptibly lowered their shoulders with satisfaction. I would start with rice and the woman would put chopstickfuls of food on top, bit by bit. First some grilled pork morsels, then a bit of spicy fried fish, then some tan xai preserved vegetables, then some fresh mint, then a fresh spring roll, then a tiny bowl of clear soup with a few torn lettuce leaves thrown in. Dishes were washed in a bowl behind the stall. Everything was scrupulously clean and ordered, even though all around was mud (it had just rained) and mayhem. A family turned up on a honda, parked it right next to the table, had a huge feast, then got on the bike and roared off again.

I wrote in my air-conditioned room but could manage only a few hours at a time as I missed the street and the market too much. I would often just walk aimlessly to see what I would see. The market was bursting with the zingy smells of fresh herbs and seafood laid out in the sun to dry. The meat department was pretty gross, unless you like goat bladders and oesophagus done three ways. Also drying in flat baskets were star anise, chillies, the brown seed pods of tamarind (delicious acid taste), peppercorns and sliced eggplant. I bought what I thought was a little bag of big green olives (well, they do grow anything in the delta) but turned out to be the most delicious marinated dates, spicy and sweet at the same time. By my third day in Can Tho, everyone I had ever bought something from, had a xe honda loi ride with or whose child I had waved to, was now my best friend. They would say 'number one lady' or give me the thumbs up or give me treats to eat. Just in case you think I'm suffering from delusions of grandeur, the Vietnamese are like this to almost everyone. All they want to do is make a connection and exchange a laugh to make the day easier. They tell lots of jokes at their own expense too and the women can be very ribald. The ones who don't say hello out of shyness, wish they had and often say it after you've gone by. The men are more reserved in general and content themselves with staring. Unique to the Mekong Delta, the xe honda loi is a thoroughly wonderful invention wherein a two-wheeled wagon/seat is attached to the dorsal fin of a motor bike. It's like a back-to-front cyclo but goes faster and the bumps hurt much more. I often saw six people and all their shopping crammed into one vehicle.

Wandering up and down the streets at right angles to the market I stopped to buy a baguette filled with sliced pork, chillies, cucumber and sauce plus three pieces of sweet potato cooked in coconut milk. This transaction caused great hilarity for some reason, as if they had just sold me gravel brochettes. I myself was in heaven and I swear to God Vietnamese baguettes are almost better than French ones. They just melt in your mouth and how they keep the crust crisp in the heat and humidity is a mystery to me. When I got back to Saigon I asked my chef friends what the secret was and they said that very little salt is used, a little sugar, half the wheat flour is substituted with rice flour and they bake many times a day, so the bread doesn't have to last. I had a beer in a bar and the professionally printed menu said, 'carry snacked' and 'sautéed snacked with satay'. This turned out to be snake. Why doesn't someone tell them there's no 'c' or 'd' in snake? Why didn't I tell them? Because I would rue the day menu translations ceased to provide so much innocent entertainment. And it doesn't happen in French. The French translations are obviously done by native French speakers and the English by someone who picked up a dictionary, drank some snake wine and hoped for the best. By the time my beer was finished, I really wanted that sautéed snacked with satay.

As I couldn't communicate with my driver Canh, I was obliged to get a guide from the nutty tourist office to accompany me in the car to the banh trang or rice paper factory. They gave me Duc again, who was in great spirits and happy to be in the vicinity of his home and his beloved family. We drove for kilometres alongside the river through idyllic, well-ordered jungle villages where life was calm and serendipitous. There were lots of little wooden bridges and a few old-style swinging monkey bridges crossing canals and streams. After half an hour we came to a bridge that was being repaired. No, we couldn't cross, the bridge was closed and yes the wait would be about five hours. We were in the middle of nowhere, a big repair truck was in the centre of the bridge and other travellers were milling around considering their options. What to do? Why, bribe of course. Duc smiled broadly, cracked a few jokes along the lines of 'if you knew how difficult she is, you wouldn't want her on this side of the bridge', greased the palm, the truck moved off the bridge, we passed, everyone waved and the truck moved back again.

We came to a traditional wooden house with shutters, which turned out to have the rice paper 'factory' out the back. This outfit was also a pig farm — an original form of cross-agriculture. Primitive would be an understatement but there in the large bamboo shed out the back, half a dozen people were making the pure white edible paper you and I swoon over when it's wrapped around some shrimp, herbs and peanuts. It is a truly magical thing to see ordinary hard old rice turn into paper sheets of translucent pastry. The rice is soaked for a couple of hours, then placed in a centrifuge. What flies out from the centrifuge is rice paste, which is put in large ceramic pots and mixed with water and salt. It's kneaded to make sure no lumps form. The paste sits in the pots for 24 hours. To make the paper, the women heat over a fire of brown rice husks huge cauldrons of water that are tightly strung with cotton cloth, like drums. A large ladle of rice flour dough is very quickly poured onto the steaming cotton surface, spread over, covered with a high lid and steamed for a few minutes. Then the lid is whipped off and the buckled white pastry deftly rolled off with a thick bamboo baton and placed on a waiting bamboo mat.

This process was very exciting for me because only last year I had been in Morocco watching the way they make their 'warka' sheet pastry. It was almost exactly the same method, except the Moroccans used a utensil like an upturned frying pan over dry heat onto which they spread a similar wettish dough made from wheat flour. I think the North Africans got this method from the Chinese (whence it originates and they also use wheat) and it was probably introduced by Marco Polo or ancient Chinese traders. Cookery writers usually tell readers to use filo pastry instead of warka but this is incorrect in my opinion. I tried won ton wrappers as a substitute; they're much closer to the consistency of warka. Beside the 'kitchen' there were high stacks of pastry-covered bamboo mats, steaming in the shade. These were then put out in the sun to dry for about four hours. That's how sheets of rice paper get their characteristic crosshatched markings – from the bamboo mats. The end result is not brittle but softly al dente and is the colour of alabaster. Now the paper can be eaten fresh like that, wrapped around things, or deep-fried. To make noodles of varying shapes and sizes, they put the steamed cold sheets through a noodle cutter and dry them in 25-centimetre lengths.

Growing rice is incredibly labour intensive and the Vietnamese women still do it all by hand as their ancestors did centuries ago. Fields are ploughed and harrowed with the help of patient water buffalo. Seeds are planted by hand and when they reach a certain age, they have to be individually uprooted and transplanted to another field to avoid root rot. Irrigation is done manually by two people swinging baskets of water on a rope from the canals to the fields. At this stage the shoots are bright green, giving the countryside its glorious colour. After six months the plants are about thigh high and sitting in 30 centimetres of water. They're ready to harvest. They look like wheat and the rice grains are contained in the fronds at the top. These are cut off by hand, then transported by wheelbarrows to threshing machines which separate the husk from the plant. I often saw brown carpets of rice drying by the side of the road, being readied for milling. The best quality rice smells slightly perfumed and herby.

Rice is the staff of life in Vietnam. Intimately entwined with the country's past, identity, culture, myth and religion, it's known as the 'pearl of the gods'. The word for rice is com, which is also the word for food, and for the casual restaurants you see everywhere. For the Vietnamese, a meal is rice and other stuff. If you haven't eaten rice then it's not a proper meal. It can be eaten brown or white, made into noodles, banh xeo (omelettes), chao (porridge), fermented into ruou gao (wine) and vinegar and the powder can be roasted. Even the rice scraped from the bottom of cooking pots is spread out on woven grass or leaf mats to dry in the sun. When it's dry it's pulverised into meal and fed to the chickens. There are rice festivals and cooking competitions. One festival in the north re-enacts the fastest way to cook rice for the battlefield. The contestants dress in traditional costume and run from a symbolic military post to the river, about a kilometre away, to fetch big bottles of water. Then they dash back and start a fire by rubbing bamboo sticks together and feeding it with straw. The raw rice must be husked with a mortar and pestle then cooked in the water over the straw fire, which must envelop the pot to ensure even cooking. The winner is the person who achieves all this first. There's no prize and I never found out if the one who eats the rice the fastest gets any kudos.

Our next stop was a place I walked through very quickly. The brochure for My Khanh 'touring village' has pictures of exotic fruit trees, lovely little lodges and animals in natural settings. It states enigmatically that 'after the long trip you will soon feel relax with fresh air of the bushes succeeding. A modern swimming pool that suits the landscape is the waiting to give tourists the most cheery minutes. You will be served quickly with the countryside meals and the southern fruits as your request. Your feasting surely more exciting with the fishes you get by yourself.' Dotted around the beautiful menagerie garden were caged animals and birds, fish in ponds, prawns in big tanks, etc. What is not stated on the brochure, what Duc refused to talk about and what the restaurant is famous for, is a walk on the wild side, a gastronomic horror show, a promenade through torture. All the animals in this garden of the devil are on the 'countryside' menu and all you have to do is point to a sun bear or maybe a bunny or a lizard or a graceful crane, and it's on your plate. Crane soup anyone? Two-flavoured bat? This place is mostly frequented by Asian men who believe that eating unusual animals will put lightning into their rods. There are so many 'aphrodisiac' foods in Vietnam (like drinking the still beating heart of a cobra in rice wine, drinking its blood and then eating its cooked flesh) that I can only assume the men have horrendous impotency problems. It's only men who partake in this macabre cruelty; it's assumed women don't need sexual powers. So after you've eaten this fear-poisoned flesh, you retire to your cute cottage to put the results to good use with the little woman, while enjoying the immeasurable pleasure of listening to other animals getting the chop all around you. Interestingly enough, I read that the demand for endangered species is down in Vietnam since the advent of Viagra. Tell that to the sun bear.

Vietnamese and other Asian gentlemen don't consume exotic food only for sexual potency. It is very expensive – monkey can cost $US300 – so being able to afford it is a sign of wealth and high social status. For example, Delacour's langur and Cat Ba langur, an Old World golden-headed monkey, are the rarest primates on earth and very highly prized. Despite the fact that they are now protected in the Cuc Phuong National Park in northern Vietnam, langurs are still illegally and heavily hunted. One-fifth of the world's most endangered primates live in Vietnam and one or more of them will become extinct in the next few decades. I'm not saying there were langurs at My Khanh; they're more likely to be eaten in the secret restaurants up north around Ha Long Bay. Someone like me, for example, would never be given crane or bat or whatever without knowing it. Such delicacies are so pricy that they're not going to waste them on an ignoramus who won't appreciate them.

Killing and eating animals who know they're about to die when you don't need to, is a form of the dangerous and spiritually bankrupt practice of 'eating fear'. This is doing something you know isn't right, like cannibalism or sinking your teeth into your lover's neck and sucking blood. Going over the line makes you feel invincible in a hallucinogenic, acid sort of way. The 'fear eaters' say they're only continuing an elaborate and obscure cultural ritual that has been going on for hundreds of years and is an intimate part of their history. In the face of modern Western revulsion at this custom, Vietnamese are both ashamed and proud. The guides pretend it doesn't happen, the staff at the zoo restaurants won't answer questions about it, especially from a woman, and the animals can't

Ga Xe Phay
Chicken Salad

Serves 6

3 tbsp lime juice
3 tbsp nuoc mam
1 tbsp rice vinegar
2 cloves garlic, minced
2 chillies, minced
2 tbsp sugar
225 g (3 cups) finely shredded Chinese cabbage
75 g (1 cup) finely shredded carrot
1 medium onion or some shallots (70 g/2$^{1}/_{2}$ oz) finely sliced
500 g (1 lb) shredded cooked chicken
$^{1}/_{2}$ cup shredded fresh mint leaves
3 tbsp chopped roasted peanuts

1 Combine the lime juice, nuoc mam, vinegar, garlic, chillies and sugar in a bowl and leave to stand for half an hour.
2 Combine the cabbage, carrot and onion in a large bowl, pour the dressing over and toss. Leave to stand for 20 minutes.
3 Add chicken and mint and toss. With your hands or serving spoons, place the salad on a beautiful platter, leaving behind excess marinade. Sprinkle the peanuts over and garnish with mint leaves.

talk. If the best way to reach a culture is through its food, then what does eating animals in this way tell us about this culture? What does it tell us about ourselves?

There's a theory that aggression and hunger are controlled by the same part of the brain, too close to each other in the hypothalamus for comfort. This is morally and intellectually slippery territory, full of contradictions and double edges. Do we think we're morally superior and socially more refined or is it just that we see cats and monkeys and bears as pets and companions, untouchable in culinary terms? In ancient Rome and Greece dogs were cooked and eaten and fish was cooked live but 'civilisation' has bred and educated these eating habits out of us. As recently as the 18th century European chefs instructed cooks to whip animals to death, insert burning irons into live pigs, pluck and roast geese alive, kick pregnant sows to death to mix their milk with their embryos. Such practices were used to tenderise the flesh, making it more succulent to eat. Furthermore, the Masai people in Kenya bleed their cows and drink the blood. And didn't we have chickens we loved in the backyard whose necks were wrung by our fathers at Christmas time? It's all very hard to understand, but not too far removed from the practice of some people even today who eat the placentas of their newborns for reasons other than the delicious taste.

My Khanh shut me down for a while and I sat sullenly in the back seat wondering if I was a hypocrite, considering how fast a beating heart might move down the oesophagus and how long it would take me to break down and eat a human if I was starving — and which bits would I start with? In contrast to my morose slouching, the boys were chatting away non-stop, happy to be alive as we bumped along jungle roads in the car, sending chickens flying and villagers waving. But you can't be dejected for long in Vietnam and it took Duc all of five minutes to think up something I would enjoy. Interrupting a rendition of 'Are You Lonesome Tonight?', he said, 'Peta, I take you to special outdoor festival of Mekong Delta food. This I know you like.'

'What special festival? When?'

'Now. Today. Near here.'

'Why didn't you tell me before?'

'Most tourist not want to see countryside and real Vietnamese food making … you very unusual … you very happy lady … you interest in everything. I think you big success story.'

'Really?'

'Yes Peta.'

'But Duc, I only experienced those things because I researched them myself. You didn't tell me about them.'

'I not tell because nobody listen. That why you success story.'

Finally Duc was coming up trumps. This culinary festival happens once a year and this weekend was the weekend. I couldn't believe my luck. It was set up outside in a pretty clearing by the river, with food trestles on one side and bamboo picnic tables under the pine trees on the other. We were treated to singing and music, wildly and enthusiastically appreciated by the punters. The only foreigner there, I feasted on beautifully, lovingly prepared fresh water crab, grilled rice paddy fish, sticky rice balls stuffed with bean paste, very fat rice noodles in coconut cream, rice paddy mouse spatchcocked and grilled (I only ate that because I thought it was a little bird but once you've eaten it, it's too late to be sick), fat juicy snails, barbecued pork and cucumber on skewers.

The best thing was the southern speciality banh xeo or to-die-for stuffed crepes. There's a lot of Indian influence in southern food, a leftover from the 14th century when the area was Indianised Khmer, and this is one of the best examples. The crepes, which are very light, crisp and lacy, are made from rice flour and coconut cream, filled with pork, shellfish and various vegetables, folded in half in the pan and served up with salad greens, herbs and nuoc mam dipping sauce. You can eat these as is or pull bits off and wrap them up. Either way it's sensational. There was a sweet breeze and pine needles floated from the trees into our food like cellophane noodles from heaven. Duc and Canh spat what they didn't want on the ground. I bristled primly every time they did it, but noticed everyone else did the same. By the time we'd finished the place looked like a bone and serviette cemetery. We left Duc at the party with his friends and drove on for four hideous, uncomfortable hours back to Saigon.

7

Da Lat

I had now learnt the long-distance-car-on-hopeless-roads lesson so booked a plane to go to Da Lat. Flying from Saigon into this town in the central highlands is like dropping into someone's backyard vegetable garden, except that it's big and mountainous and green. From the air the ordered European-style gardens are like handkerchiefs spread out around the valleys. The long drive from the airport squashed into the shuttle bus gives you plenty of time to enjoy the beautiful streams, lakes and waterfalls and place personal bets on how fast the driver can hurtle around blind bends. The countryside is not at all tropical, but more like pastoral France or New Zealand, with curvaceous, rolling hills and fertile, free-draining valleys. In fact, it's called the city of eternal spring. Da Lat is an old colonial hill retreat, established in 1920, favoured by the French and the last emperor Bao Dai because of its lush, tranquil surroundings and fresh mountain air; a respite for government officials from the clotting heat of Saigon. Upon arrival in the town I inspected three hotels for the usual requirements before I found something suitable. It was more suitable than I could afford but every so often one tires of noisy charm and longs for a gorgeous bathroom with wooden shutters and a pretty garden. This I found at the Empress, a small 'boutique' hotel with outdoor dining and copies of French masters on the walls. The amazing thing about Da Lat, which strikes you immediately, is that it's not hot; you're not sweating. Visitors don't look like dead ducks there; they look relaxed and well adjusted.

My hotel was on the man-made Lake Xuan Huong in the heart of the town, surrounded by low hills, villas and pine forests. I donned my trusty blue plastic raincoat and took a little stroll into town. Downtown Da Lat was not at all what I was expecting. From my research I had envisaged a cute provincial French town, with great cafés, French-speaking people and the charm of somewhere like Hoi An. But Da Lat is filthy, like a lot of Vietnamese towns, and it's rather Wild West, like a mountain town in Mexico with very savage looking, dark-skinned people. I don't mean wild in the ferocious sense, but in the natural untrammelled sense. You couldn't find a place or people more unlike Hoi An if you tried. The people in the markets in Da Lat don't look like anyone else in Vietnam and if they resemble rustic hill tribes who have just come down from the mountains it's because they have. They're minority ethnic groups who even call themselves the French word for it – montagnards. Although it's not cold, the inhabitants obviously think it is and wrap up dementedly against the cool weather of 25°C. They tramp around in the mud (it's raining) in gumboots, pants, hand-knitted sweaters, jackets and conical hats, knitted hats or even fur hats. I'm dressed in shirt and pants and am perfectly comfortable, blissfully comfortable. Avoiding sweating for a few days is a good enough reason to be in Da Lat. Because I'm in the highlands, the temperature is always between a cool 15°C (59°F) and perfect 25°C (77°F). When I told people in Saigon I was going to Da Lat they acted as though I was going to the South Pole and said, 'Oooh, you'll have to buy a jacket.' People actually come on shopping expeditions to Da Lat to buy warm clothing because they can't get it anywhere else in the south.

The large market in the middle of hilly Da Lat town is like a southern French covered market on two levels – well, three really but there's no food on the top storey, only clothes and very ugly trash. For the flower

COM
RICE

Vietnamese don't usually wash their rice and they like it very dry. Salt is never added. This is a good guide for rice/water ratio:

1 cup rice = $1^1/_2$ cups water to cook for 20 minutes
2 cups rice = $2^1/_2$ cups water to cook for 25 minutes
3 cups rice = $3^1/_2$ cups water to cook for 30 minutes

A Chinese clay pot is the best thing to cook rice in. Glazed black/brown inside and unglazed off white outside, it has little handles and is encased in a wire frame. When the pot is new, fill it with water and place in a medium oven till half the water evaporates. Allow it to air dry and it's ready to use. Start cooking on a low heat and gradually raise it. Don't put the pot on heat empty – it must have liquid or food in it. If you're using an electric stove, always use a diffuser. To clean the pot, rub the interior with salt and run hot water over it.

Serves 6 to 8 – makes 6 cups
2 cups long grain rice (Thai jasmine is the best outside Vietnam)
Chinese clay pot or heavy-based saucepan

1   Place rice in the clay pot, add the water and bring to the boil. Give the rice a stir and reduce the heat to the lowest it will go, cover the pot and go away without touching or lifting the lid, till the time is up.
2   Remove from the heat without lifting the lid and let stand for 10 minutes. Stir with a wooden spoon a few times and serve.

department, which is at the front, peasants arrive from the country with gigantic bundles of chrysanthemums and hydrangeas wrapped in huge flax mats, balanced on their bikes. You must walk past and through this bursting display of colour and perfumes to get into the interior. If you're standing on the first-floor balcony looking down to the ground floor, the view is heart-warming – like a tapestry of brightly coloured vegetable and fruit stalls lined up à la Française. Also the produce on sale is different, for Da Lat is one of the vegetable and fruit growing areas of Vietnam and they grow things no one else can, such as white and green asparagus, avocados and artichokes. They make an artichoke tea there which is very refreshing with a drip of lime and one restaurant I went to had no less than 24 fresh fruits listed on its menu.

There are European fruit and vegetables here – strawberries, mulberries, tomatoes, little pumpkins, pink garlic, pink Heritage potatoes, pink shallots, leeks, spring onions, garlic onions, baby bananas, pale pale okra, peas, carrots, green beans, chokos, beetroot. I hadn't seen a beetroot since I'd been in Vietnam. The tiny artichokes have a delicate sweet flavour. They produce little waste because they don't have the tough choke you have to remove from the bigger varieties. Although they're usually called baby artichokes, these small flowers aren't young, immature specimens that would eventually grow to full size if they were left on the plant. Nor are they a different species. They're fully grown siblings of the main (large) artichoke on each stem. (Incidentally, artichokes aren't really a vegetable; they're the bud of a flower and related to the thistle family.) Upstairs on the first-floor balcony are dozens of open restaurants, some vegetarian, some fish and some meat, all full all day with families happily stuffing themselves. At the back of the market is the scary meat department, all sorts of innards, pig's ears and tails, and fish stalls weighed down with the catch from Nha Trang on the coast – tuna, bream, blue crab, prawns and lots of dried fish and seafood. At the very back and on a sort of mezzanine floor, the poor birds are crammed into cages awaiting their particular fates, all of which involve a cleaver and loss of face.

Around the square in front of the market there are delicious food stalls which, like a fire in the lounge, appear only at night and are just as comforting. Large pots of seafood in coconut milk, vermicelli and beef soups different from pho but just as good, grilling pork and chicken, shellfish which is steamed open and served on large platters in the shell with side sauces, pots of rice on every stall and dau hu, a pudding made from sugar, soy milk and fresh ginger. Da Lat food is hearty, not sophisticated like Saigon food and, because it's so 'cold' there they eat lots of congee. Normally this is an unappetising rice gruel like porridge but the Da Lat version is absolutely delicious. They cook it in pork broth with bits of pork meat and ginger and garlic, then serve it up topped with chilli oil, fried shallots and coriander. My hotel also made a chicken and a vegetarian one which I alternated for breakfast every day. Sometimes the good stall holders get it very wrong, though. One day I sat down to fish with coconut juice thinking they meant milk. But no, it was thickened juice – a bit like eating fried cardboard with glue.

The real secret of Da Lat, however, is that this town and its surroundings are full of nutty, eccentric, avant garde people who live there for the cool climate, small town charm and beautiful surroundings. I set out in my sensible shoes and raincoat to find some of them. The first nutty place in the centre of town is the Tang Café, a small, dim, subversive coffee bar in the old sense of the word. Reliable sources say neither the decor nor the menu has changed one iota since the 1970s and I believe them. Everything is brown, the tables are low, everyone is smoking and they only serve drinks like artichoke tea and coffee. There's no food whatsoever and the music is soft jazz. It reminded me of another, younger self with long black wavy hair, pale pink lipstick, black tights and baggy sweater. I almost felt the need to chirp something from my old Joan Baez songbook. Fortunately I saved that impulse for a much more auspicious occasion – the day I met the moustachioed poet, Duy Viet.

STOP and GO. It's a haiku.

DALAT = Dak Aliis Latitiem Aliis Temperiem.

This is the kind of esoteric information you're given when you get into a conversation with the guys at the famous Stop and Go Café. I was lucky to get into a conversation with them at all as when I turned up at the unbohemian hour of 10 a.m., no one was at the café. My honda om gentleman, Loi, had driven me up a street straight out of rural France in the 1930s and down a driveway to the new location of the Stop and Go. It used to be a funky, dark café above the central market, fulminating with left-wing intent, and was the hangout for poets, painters and musicians in the 1970s and it still is – the 1970s, that is. The art gallery/café is now on the ground floor of Duy Viet's pink-washed French-style mansion surrounded by lush plants, flowers and sculptures. An old woman is sweeping and a toddler is playing with a puppy and a kitten. I'm the only customer so I order a Vietnamese coffee and wander into the main room furnished with comfortable bamboo chairs and couches, tables covered in books of poetry, magazines and visitors' books bulging with messages, photos, poems and drawings. It appears that no one who comes here can resist literary self-expression inspired by the moody environment. From famous French chefs to John Kennedy to movie stars to writers to ordinary visitors, all have been enthralled to find themselves in a time capsule. In the corner under the wooden stairs leading to the living quarters upstairs, sits a desk covered in papers, poems, ink and brushes. The walls are covered from top to bottom in paintings and calligraphic poems. All is slightly European/tropical/faded/avant-garde and you can think of certain friends who would absolutely love this place and others who wouldn't understand it at all.

> Sipping coffee on a bourgeois Monday
> over the market.
> Warmed by coals,
> I indulge in the illusion
> that I am here
> and that I can,
> with wine days behind me,
> repaint the picture
> they painted for me, until
> in the rain
> under a shared umbrella,
> you tell me I am wrong.
> Smaller now,
> I return to my easel.
> Tearing off another leaf,
> I add it slowly to the fire

that burns inside me
and is just now learning
how to rage
with each new day.
Duy Viet, July 1992

I wrote Duy Viet a note saying I would come back and was just leaving
the café when the very man pulled up on a honda. A small, slim, aged man
got off, the woman rushed over and said there's a writer here to see you and
it was all go. He was dressed in solid shoes and socks, nicely pressed
trousers, shirt, vest, tweed coat, French beret and moustache. He was so
much as I expected him to be that I wanted to hug him with delight.
Speaking French, he begged me to sit down, offered me a cigarette, and
because the mood demanded it, I smoked it with great pleasure. Duy Viet
was accompanied by a friend who was dressed exactly the same. They both
spoke perfect French and were thoroughly versed in French literature,
interspersing quotations throughout our conversation. Their names are
literary pseudonyms; I know his friend Viet Trang's real name is Pham Gia
Triep, but I never found out Duy Viet's. They were both very bright and
friendly and generous with their time. I bought a calligraphic poem from
Duy Viet which said, in English, 'Love makes time pass, time makes love
pass.' When I asked where the name Stop and Go came from, Viet Trang
wrote this in my notebook:

Terre des hommes n'est q'une auberge
Merveilleusement Créateur en dispose.
Tout individu n'est q'un passant
S'arrêtant puis s'en allant ...

The earth is just a haven for man
Marvellously laid out by God.
Everyone is just passing through
Stopping and then going ...

I asked Duy Viet to sing a song and he took a rusty old guitar down from the wall. I had assumed it was there only as decoration but when he began playing, it was perfectly in tune. He sang romantic songs in English and French which he had composed himself. He was a journalist in another life and has three children, one of whom I met. Minh (pronounced 'Ming') writes news for the local television station. She speaks English, but not French, which is how it is in Vietnam now. The older people speak French and take great pleasure in doing so, but the younger people speak only English. The old woman was his wife and spoke only Vietnamese. The two gentlemen were in their late 70s and Viet Trang told me he has 12 children. I gasped and mentioned the powers of snake wine but he assured me he'd managed it all on his own. Before 1975 he was a civil servant in the old government and earned a good wage. He maintains he has been unemployed since 1975 and supported by his wife who makes noodles for all the restaurants around town. Her speciality is wheat flour pasta to satisfy Da Lat's taste for spaghetti Bolognese! Nine of his children still live around him in Da Lat. As I was leaving, he wrote this poem in my notebook:

Prochaine Rencontre
Puisque notre merveilleuse planete est ronde
Puisque la fleur parfumé se fane et s'épanouit
Puisque la belle lune s'éclipse et reluit
Nous nous serons la main
Prochaine rencontre.

The Next Meeting
Since our wonderful planet is round
Since a perfumed flower fades and blooms
Since the beautiful moon waxes and wanes
We will shake hands
Till the next meeting.

SUP MANG TAY NAU CUA
ASPARAGUS AND CRAB SOUP

This classic example of French Vietnamese fusion originally used canned French asparagus with fresh crab meat. These days the Vietnamese have learnt how to grow asparagus in Da Lat so you often find it made with the fresh product. If you're feeling very lethargic, use canned crab meat (never frozen), but it's truly much more fragrant with fresh crab.

Serves 4 to 6

1 litre (4 cups) chicken stock (home-made if possible)

$^1/_2$ tsp sugar

2 tbsp nuoc mam

250 g (2 cups) fresh asparagus spears, trimmed and cut into 3 cm (1 in) sections

1 tbsp vegetable oil

6 shallots (about 100 g/3$^1/_2$ oz) finely chopped

2 cloves of garlic, finely minced

freshly ground black pepper and sea salt to taste

150 g (1 cup) fresh (or canned) crab meat

2 tbsp cornflour mixed with 2 tbsp cold water

1 lightly beaten egg

finely chopped spring onion and coriander for garnish

1   Bring the chicken stock, sugar and nuoc mam to the boil, throw in the asparagus and simmer gently till asparagus is cooked through.

2   While this is happening, gently sauté the shallots and garlic in the oil for about 5 minutes.

3   Add shallots, garlic, pepper, salt and crab meat to the soup and simmer for a few minutes.

4   Add the cornflour and simmer for a few minutes till soup has thickened a little then slowly pour in the beaten egg and stir. Beautiful threads will form.

To serve: Divide the soup into 4 or 6 bowls and garnish with spring onions and coriander.

They advised me that the best restaurant in town was Long Hoa where I could eat Madame Pham's pasta and parlez-vous with Renée, the Vietnamese owner. Viet Trang walked me all the way there, then turned around and walked home again. This was a family-run restaurant with a room at the front and another room at the back, separated by a kitchen. The room at the back was great – piano, couches for lounging around on and more ornate table settings. A sign on the wall said, 'Tout repas est festin lorsque l'amitié le sert' (every meal is a feast as long as it's with friends). The best part of the meal was the yoghurt served in little glass jars shaped like old-fashioned milk cans. It was thick and rich and tasted slightly of strawberries. Strawberries are one of the fruits for which Da Lat is famous and their cooks make fabulous thick jam, wine, extracts for syrups and tea (skills learned from the French). Fresh, luscious strawberries are for sale everywhere, as are mulberries, grapes, blackcurrants, plums and peaches, which they also candy and dry. The food stalls are bulging with bright packets full of these flavour bursts.

In the drizzling afternoon, I jumped on the back of Loi's honda om and went off to visit the Hang Nga Guest-house and Art Gallery, otherwise known as the 'crazy house' by locals. This place is really hard to describe, unless you're related to Salvador Dali or Gaudi or tripping on acid. There are giant wire spiderwebs in the real trees, fake trees made of concrete and chicken wire which contain bedrooms with glass ceilings so you can look up into real trees, caves, sculptures, a tearoom inside a giraffe, an outdoor art gallery with paintings sitting in the rain and a café. The designer of all this, Madame Dang Viet Nga (called Hang Nga), lives in a French villa on the property and there's a sort of museum room and altar dedicated to her parents. Her father, Truong Chinh, took over from Ho Chi Minh as Vietnam's second president from 1981 till his death in 1988. Hang Nga was brought up in Hanoi and obtained a PhD in architecture from the University of Moscow where she lived for 14 years. She is very avant-garde, dresses in 1970s hippy clothes, flared pants, long wavy hair et al, speaks in a soft, mysterious voice and burns incense. The counter-culture is alive and well. This woman is a national treasure and should be loved and protected at all costs.

By and large it's only foreigners who appreciate Hang Nga's work, which is so kitsch it's fabulous. The locals are either afraid of it or think it's mad. Their taste for kitsch is completely different and in Da Lat runs more to stuffed animals, mini-zoos, people dressed as rabbits, bears and cowboys, an imitation Eiffel Tower, artificial waterfalls and lakes with hideous rowboats and junk kiosks. Vietnamese tourists and honeymooners love this ghastly stuff and they flock to the third floor at the market which is crammed to the ceiling with unadulterated rubbish and anything that shines or sparkles. Particularly attractive are the wood carvings like those old tree stump clocks you used to buy in the 1970s. When I asked hoteliers about the Hang Nga Guest-house they told me it's a ghastly place where you never get any peace and best just to visit (which you have to pay for, by the way). The People's Committee puts up with it only because it's now a tourist attraction and Hang Nga's impressive parentage gives her lots of pull. There used to be another masterpiece called the 'House with a Hundred Roofs' which they destroyed because it looked 'anti-socialist'. Hang Nga has designed other buildings around Da Lat, including the Catholic church in Lien Khuong and the Children's Cultural Palace.

The last person on my list of desirable eccentrics was the solitary monk at the Lam Ty Ni Pagoda. The honda om bumped and scraped in the rain along the horrendous road to the pagoda. Loi and I got off at the large, decorative front gate and walked up the path through flower beds and gardens to the temple. There were Japanese gardens with a little bridge, hanging pots, trellises and wooden furniture, all created by the busy monk Vien Thuc. The huge, ebony doors of the pagoda were closed so we knocked long and loud because he's always there but way out the back in his art studio. Eventually the door was opened by a small man with a big smile and intelligent eyes, dressed in brown robes, holey socks and a woolly cap with flaps. He greeted Loi like an old friend and they began chatting, leaving me to wander around. We removed our shoes to walk through the temple, then put them on again to go out to the studio. There I found two German girls colouring in pictures Thuc had drawn to raise money for the Children's Cultural Palace. I walked through numerous large rooms neatly crammed with literally thousands of paintings and haiku poems, lined up against the walls, hanging from hooks by coloured string and lying in piles.

When I got back to the studio, Thuc had his feet up in one of his hand-made chairs and was firing questions about me at Loi. The trees and flowers were dripping around us and I asked him to write me a poem. He grabbed my notebook and quickly wrote, 'Walking along the longest path of the world searching for the book of my heart', then did a drawing of his hooded head on the opposite page, wrote 'Happy memories in the trip will last forever when being home again' and signed it. Not for nothing is he now known as the business monk by locals – his instant art is prolific, which is not to say worthless. Picasso did lots of copies and even had a factory producing his ceramic pieces, so I've nothing against capitalism in art. It's just incongruous in a ragtag monk who needs a good bath and is supposed to be a penniless hermit.

He's said to be the wealthiest person in Da Lat but the Vietnamese are terrible gossips so of course I took no notice of this. The locals whisper that he's a hypocrite and a fraud but I say if you can found a pagoda in 1961 and stay in it on your own for all those years being very productive, more power to you. This guy has so many visitors and is so social and quick in the English, French, Khmer and Thai languages that he hardly has time to pray. He maintains he finally gets around to praying at 4 a.m., eats only fruit and paints the rest of the time. Thuc was educated at Da Lat University, is highly intelligent and witty and is world famous thanks to foreigners' utter fascination with him. He's the sort of person you could have a good rave with for hours. I asked him to paint a poem in Vietnamese on a long strip of paper and he wrote 'golden words near rocky wall' over a swish of colour and charged me US$5. He had wads of money in his shirt beneath his robe and I expressed the hope that he was putting it all in the bank. 'Oh yes, indeed I am,' he replied. 'I want to visit my friends all over the world where all my paintings are hanging and I will get there one day. I have already been to Thailand and Cambodia.' He walked us to the door of his studio and said goodbye, then walked us to the door of the temple and said goodbye, then walked us to the big gate and said goodbye. I liked him.

On the way home we passed the colourful Cao Dai church blessed with a bizarre mix of architectural styles – Catholic church, pagoda, theme park and village hall with a distinct predilection for dragons and snakes. The Cao Dai religion was very political and very powerful from the 1920s till 1975 but has died down to a certain extent; there are about three million followers at present. Invented by a Hanoi civil servant, it is a fusion of secular and religious philosophies from both East and West, an effort to be the ideal religion where all truths are reconciled and truth is love. There are Mahayana Buddhist, Taoist, Confucian and Catholic influences. All sorts of colourful people 'speak' to Cao Dai followers, including Mohammed, Jesus, Moses and even Victor Hugo and William Shakespeare. The Cao Dai temples are pale blue and pink and have the religion's official symbol, the 'divine eye' above the altar. There are female cardinals and even a pope. When Graham Greene was in Vietnam he was very taken by this religion and almost converted but eventually found the priests a little too cunning and corrupt for his taste. He wrote about their festivals at the Holy See in Tay Ninh, outside Saigon in the 1950s. These festivals, held on any pretext, mainly to keep the people enthralled, enjoyed high-profile political guests from the government and army. The French Foreign Legion, mostly composed of famously vicious Moroccans and Senegalese, ran the security in the surrounding countryside and everyone nervously turned up from Saigon in big official cars, anxious to be seen and get out again before the 7 p.m. curfew.

My guide Loi was becoming more and more friendly and asked me out to dinner that night. I politely declined, saying I had to write. He found out my room number and called me a few times, wanting to know if I had changed my mind. No I hadn't, thank you. I was slightly perturbed that he had been given my room number and they were putting him through directly. It was also surprising to have a guide cross the line like that, as Vietnamese men are generally very polite and not interested in middle-aged travelling women, even if they do look a bit outlandish. The next morning I kept my arrangement with him to take me into the hills to visit a minority Lat tribe village. Nothing was mentioned. He had hired his friend's car as I didn't fancy bumping around the countryside on a honda in the pouring rain. One can't just take it into one's head to visit a minority village. One can't even pass through these places on the way to somewhere else without permission. Permission cost $US5 and then we were on our way to the hamlets of the mysterious, dark-skinned Lat (as in Da Lat because they were the original inhabitants and Da means river), at the base of Lang Bien Mountain about 12 kilometres north of Da Lat. Only 50 years ago this and other mountains in the area were thick with forests full of game such as wild oxen, boar, deer, elephants, rhinoceroses, hares and tigers. Now they are defoliated and because the French were such good hunters, all these animals are now extinct.

As we drove through the pretty countryside, Loi explained Lat traditions to me. Originally their houses were built on stilts with rough wooden walls and thatched roofs. Their animals lived underneath. Now, however, they are forbidden to live like this because the authorities consider it dirty. When my friend Mel was filming her adventure travel show in the north, the crew stayed in one of these stilt houses, sleeping on the floor. In the middle of the night Mel woke up and saw a heavily pregnant woman coming toward her in the dark. She went to where Mel was lying, pulled up her skirt, squatted down right next to her pillow and peed into a hole in the floor, which was obviously the toilet. The urine (and excrement) went directly on top of the pigs underneath. By this stage the others were awake and silently screaming; for the rest of the night they took turns staying awake to keep people away from the toilet. Ah, what you do for a good story. The Lat are Catholic and have interesting matriarchal marriage agreements. The husband gives a dowry to the wife, he leaves his home to live in hers and works for her and her family. The children take her name and if she dies, he has to marry her sister.

The Lat speak a dialect and keep very much to themselves. Until recently they were severely underprivileged and looked down upon by the Vietnamese majority who didn't even consider them to be Vietnamese, although legally they are and, what's more, they're indigenous. The locals forced them to produce charcoal, a contemptible, filthy job, and today they're still pretty poor, scratching out a living growing rice, corn, pumpkins, tobacco and sometimes cotton. In contrast to the north, where montagnards are left alone, the government strictly controls minority tribes in the central highlands. Only as recently as 1992 the central highlands and minority villages were closed to outsiders. They have been known to stick up for themselves in the past by creating the fearsome guerilla band FULRO (United Front for the Struggle of the Oppressed Races) and during the war helped the Americans against the Communist Vietnamese. The party has never forgiven them for this so they are 'helping' to Vietnamise them by 'planting' Vietnamese settlers in their territories, replacing their traditional slash and burn agriculture with fixed place farming and kindly opening schools and printing textbooks in Vietnamese, which is not their language and which they can't read.

The best thing the Lat women produce is their stunning weaving. We stopped at an open wooden shed where scarves, bedspreads and mats were on sale, exchanged a few little bows with the women and sat down on dolly stools to dolly cups of tea. Sitting on mats on the hard mud floor, two young women were creating the most refined, lyrical patterns and colour combinations from looms they had strapped themselves into. They passed a band around their backs and secured it, and pressed their feet up against blocks of wood to keep their bodies steady. Using eight slats, magical fingers and generations of learning, centimetre by centimetre, silk and cotton fabric emerged. I bought a large burnt orange cotton bedspread overwoven with pale gold and chocolate silk threads, bordered by a 5-centimetre orange cotton band overwoven with green and white silk. This masterpiece cost $US20. After caressing every one of the dozens of scarves hanging on racks around the shed, I finally chose a searing turquoise blue one with an orange and navy blue plaid pattern and long silk tassels. We walked around the muddy village in the light drizzle. The people wear a mixture of Lat and Vietnamese clothing and the women carry babies in blankets on their backs. Old women have bamboo pierced ears with huge heavy earrings hanging from them and smoke pipes. This village won my prize for the best spitters; even the children could cover really long distances.

Almost every house had a vegetable garden and chickens and we visited a traditional wooden show home. There were musical instruments and wooden gongs hanging on the wall, used to call the villagers when there's a party on. And it seems that any excuse for a party is a good one because (a) you get to hang out with your mates and (b) you get to drink home-made hooch called ruou can. Reasons for a party include religion, births, deaths, weddings, important guests, full moon, harvest, new house, happiness, sadness. Ruou can means straw liquor. A can is a straw made from a long, slim, elegant bamboo, slightly bent, and is used to suck the ruou up out of its large clay pot or che. It's a communal thing — you sit around the pot with your friends and everyone sucks. This is interspersed with eating, dancing, singing and storytelling till everyone is completely drunk. Ruou is made from sticky rice which is soaked overnight. In the morning you add rice husks and steam the mixture to a thick soupy gloop. Then you add water and yeast made from cardamom leaves, put it into the che, cover it and go away for two weeks. When you come back it's time for a party.

It was raining hard, I was back in my room overlooking the lake, I'd had the gin and tonic and a wee siesta to the calming sound of the rain falling. The temperature had gone down a little so all those montagnards wrapped up in woolly hats, gumboots and padded jackets would be happy. I was wrapped in my new orange bedspread and writing with the door open so I could watch the light change. It was 6.15 p.m. and darkness had already fallen unobtrusively save for the tinkling of the burst clouds. At 10.30 p.m. the phone rang. Foolishly I answered it. Loi. No thanks. Half an hour later the phone rang again. Loi was downstairs and wanted to come up. No thanks and go away. Ten minutes later, a knock at the door.

Loi wanted to come in. I shrieked that I was in bed for God's sake and was a tragic widow and too old for him and would he please leave me alone. I went back to bed and realised my hands were trembling. It was borderline stalking. Easy for Nancy Reagan to advise 'just say no' but she's obviously never met a lovesick mountain bachelor in her travels. I was due to stay another day but by morning had decided enough was enough and I was out of there. I changed my flight back to Saigon and jumped on the airport shuttle. In the meantime Loi had discovered my dastardly ruse and just as we pulled out of the pickup area from another hotel on the way, I saw him drive in, ask a few questions and stare after the shuttle. At that point he must have decided I wasn't worth following and drove off.

Heavens, I thought, this is not very comme il faut.

8

Saigon again

I'm back at the Continental, it's six o'clock on Sunday night and the nuttiest passegiata in the world has begun. I open the windows of my room on to Dong Khoi Street and watch the sky turn murky blue then cobalt then indigo then black in the rain, illuminated by lightning and thunderstruck by crashing clouds. This does nothing to dampen the spirits of the bikers for their ritual is beyond weather — it's something they have to do. There's no point to it, they don't stop and talk to each other, they're going nowhere. It's all for show. Everyone is dressed up, the girls riding side-saddle showing off their beautiful legs, the boys in check shirts, with combed hair. Not unlike an exercycle, the passegiata Saigonais has no destination but you have the illusion of having achieved something and everyone is satiated. Maybe what you've achieved is the sweet pleasure of being very close in a mobile embrace with your beau, whispering forbidden nothings in his ear.

Alice and the cousin were going out to her country house at Long An, west of Saigon, and invited me to come along. She was anxious for me to see her home place — what she called Vietnam profonde. She wanted to show me what sort of life she had come from and how beautiful the land was, so I would understand about the past. Long An is famous for growing rice, coconuts and the sweetest pineapples in Vietnam. We rode in one of the cousin's flashest vans with chauffeur, air-con that worked and cushions to put our feet on. The cousin – long black hair in a big, shining bun at the base of her neck, pale pink linen pants, white linen blouse, dark red nail polish and diamond and jade jewellery – remained polite but stand-offish with me. She and Alice talked non-stop with the driver while I enjoyed the brilliant green rice paddies, pineapple plantations and clear blue skies and thought, I must change my nail polish and get some more diamonds.

We turned into Alice's property, past rice paddies into the drive and up to a large house with a very grand entrance surrounded by fountains, sculptured bonsai gardens and trees. Alice was not impressed to see the Communist flag flying at the front of the house, it being National Day. 'The flag is by obligation, not by choice, I can assure you, Peta,' she sniffed. This is what is astonishing about the Vietnamese. Adaptable and pragmatic, they just go along with things to keep the peace but they never change underneath. They remain who they are – French-speaking Catholics or Buddhists or whatever – but if the local party is going to make a fuss, they'll fly the flag. We were ushered into the house and brought delicious drinks of chanh day with oodles of rice. In order to make ends meet, the women of the household had turned the property into an outdoor bar. Little eating and drinking areas, sheltered by palm leaf roofs, were dotted around the gardens. The house, a shadow of its former glory, had huge bedrooms with en suites and cheap furnishings, a wide hallway, a large indoor kitchen and, separated by a sort of dining room, the outdoor kitchen.

The woman doing most of the cooking was a family friend called Minh, who spoke perfect French and was thrilled to be able to communicate with me when the others had trouble. She told me chanh day meant lime lemons but then where did the black seeds in the drink come from? I followed her into the outdoor kitchen where I stayed, nattering to her and the sisters, sitting on the steps in the corner, till lunch was served. She showed me the lime lemons, which turned out to be large passion-fruit. Alice and the cousin's sole purpose for being there seemed to be to talk to the family, lie down and fan themselves and take naps. We were there all day and whenever I couldn't find them in the huge mansion, I just had to look into a bedroom and there they were, changed from city linens into country cottons, asleep on a bed.

There were women and children cousins of all ages (the men work in the city and were nowhere to be seen) and I found out why Alice has so many cousins and half-sisters. Her wealthy father had several wives and mistresses, all of whom produced children, all of whom had the right to live on this property. There were photos of father in a suit, sitting with his legs crossed and staring straight at the camera, handsome and confident. Next to them, photos of his parents in traditional dress, looking seriously at the camera. An older sister had obviously had a different life from Alice as she spoke only Vietnamese and had betel stained black teeth. But they were all beautiful and all looked very alike, in spite of having different mothers. Older sister was busy in the inside kitchen partitioning boiled duck, making patties out of the blood and poaching them in the broth, then cooking sticky rice in the broth. Outside, Minh was frying chao tom ground shrimp on sugar cane sticks. The smell was driving me insane. The girls were making up all sorts of peculiar beverages for the young people who zoomed into the garden on their bikes to have a drink, listen to loud music and zoom off again — glasses of yoghurt full of ice and lemon wedges and glasses of condensed milk full of ice with pots of iced tea on the side which they poured into the drinks and mixed around. They banged the ice off a large suitcase-sized block kept in a cool box.

Finally it was lunchtime and we sat under the trees to eat the prawn paste off the sticks, then suck on the sweet sugar cane underneath. As is usual in Vietnam, there were plates of greens and herbs and lots of paper serviettes. The duck dish I saw big sister preparing in the kitchen was called chao vit, a typical country recipe that Alice assured me I would be hard put to find in a restaurant. The cut up duck was served on a plate

Nuoc Cot Dua
Fresh Coconut Milk

When buying a coconut, shake it up to your ear to make sure there's fluid in it. If you can't hear water sloshing around, the coconut is old and dry inside.

Makes about 2 cups

1 coconut
3 cups of milk
large piece of cheesecloth
medium sieve
a bowl

1   Crack the coconut open, remove the flesh with the point of a heavy knife. For making coconut milk, you don't need to peel the skin off. Coarsely grate the flesh or cut it into little pieces and whiz in the food processor for about 30 seconds.
2   Bring the milk to the boil. Pour half the milk into the processor and blend for 30 seconds. Leave to sit for half an hour.
3   Line the sieve with the cheesecloth and place over a bowl. Pour in the coconut milk. Bring together the edges of the cheesecloth and squeeze out as much milk into the bowl as possible.
4   Put the coconut flesh back in the processor and repeat this process with the rest of the milk.
5   Throw out the coconut flesh and combine the 2 milks. Now you can use it or keep it in the fridge for not more than a few days. Once it's refrigerated, the fat will rise to the top. I like it, so stir it back in, but you can scrape it off if you wish.

with its ginger dipping sauce, surrounded by fresh mint and pickled vegetables, and the soup was garnished with chopped liver and the blood patties. We sprinkled on freshly grated ginger, spring onions and lots of aromatic black pepper. The women took this feast seriously, grabbing pieces of duck and eating with their lacquered fingertips till every last drop and morsel was gone. Alice fished good bits out with chopsticks and put them in my bowl. And all the time we were drinking and drinking – water, tea and beer. Afterwards we had segments of pomelo (like giant grapefruit but sweeter) and lumps of blood-red watermelon. Alice encouraged me to dip the pomelo in salt and chilli which, amazingly, completely changed the flavour. We went inside and lay around on couches in the living room and Alice began talking about her family.

'My grandfather was the mayor of this area and a wealthy landowner. The family owned all the land around here, all of which we have lost. During the civil war, the Communists forced him to feed and look after their troops. It was disgusting having these ignorant people in the beautiful old house, treating them like servants. They ruined things in the house, had no respect and plundered the land around. When the French found out about this, to punish my grandfather, they mercilessly bombed Long An and the house, completely destroying it. Most of the family escaped to Saigon. The house we're in now is the second house, built on the ruins of the first. Then in 1940 the Japanese took over and my father had to deal with them. My mother was very beautiful and the wife my father was truly in love with but he couldn't be faithful and she finally got sick of it and left.

My first husband was 20 years older than me, very wealthy and the marriage was more or less arranged. I didn't love him. My second husband was the great love of my life, also wealthy. I had my dress designing business and created a centre for handicapped women. When we escaped to Paris two days before the fall with our four children, of course I lost almost everything and I have no idea what happened to those poor women.'

Alice's family of lovely women were endlessly concerned with my comfort. If I moved to scratch a foot, anti-mosquito cream would appear; if I fluttered my pink fan, they moved me into an air-conditioned room; if my ankles looked swollen, a chair and cushion would be drawn up to put my feet on; if I sweated they set up a table with drinks beside me till I had a line-up of beer, tea, coffee and water in a thermos flask. They were such beautiful, soft people that it was almost sad to leave them in the dusk. Everyone lined up in the driveway, from babies to grandmothers, kissing us goodbye and shaking hands. I left money for the children and they all came up to me one by one and bowed shyly. Minh's eyes were shining as she hugged me – I don't think they often receive such visitors from the outside world. As we drove out we waved to a smiling cousin and his family who were given the property next door by Alice's father after the American war. Once aristocrats, they now grow rice. Three days later, this man's teenage daughter was dead, killed in a motor cycle accident.

Alice could always be relied upon to turn up with culinary experiences at either end of the scale – all I had to do was ask. In fact I didn't even have to ask. Like most Vietnamese, once she'd discovered my interest, she keep coming up with original and diverse ways to satisfy it. Alice was just as happy with a cheap pho in the suburbs as she was in expensive downtown restaurants like the Hoi An. On this occasion, she got her driver revved up on a Sunday morning and we set off for the countryside through insane traffic and ugly towns to the village of Binh Thanh. After 8 kilometres we suddenly turned left off the road, leaving behind the noisy, messy village, and passed down a long, coconut palmed drive. This opened out like a panoramic movie to a very ritzy outdoor restaurant in spectacular grounds. They call these places 'villages'. They were like the ones I visited in the Mekong Delta but without exotic animals and much more upmarket. The main house was decorated with dark sea-green cane couches, fans, Italian tiles, thick bamboo blinds, antiques and people in white linen draped around the bar. There was a huge French-style kitchen anyone in the South-west of France would be proud of. Nothing happened there. The real action was in the long outdoor kitchen attached to it. Wealthy Vietnamese always have the flash show kitchen but most of the actual cooking goes on outside, just as happened during my time in India when the maid eschewed the modern kitchen to cook her rice on a fire in the garden shed, and in Morocco where a house had three fully equipped kitchens but all the cooking was done on the roof over braziers. This one was a true outside Vietnamese kitchen with rows of burners and lots of chopping going on.

This serene and bucolic property was graced with a mini-golf range, tropical gardens of birds of paradise, bougainvillaea and hibiscus, lily ponds and wooden, palm-thatched open-sided huts decorated with watermelon-pink and cucumber-green furniture. These structures had bamboo blinds so that, if it rained, all one had to do was let them down and keep sipping. Some of the huts were bars, some reclining areas and the largest was a restaurant. Alice and I arranged ourselves prettily in a pergola by the Saigon River which bordered the property. She was dressed in an elegant leaf-green linen trouser suit, Chanel handbag and full make-up in the heat; I was in a slash of crimson lipstick and the famous lime-green, red-piped Chinese pants and top for which the Hanoi seamstress had merrily told me I was far too old. I took great pleasure in wearing this outfit as the fine silk was deliciously cool and if you found yourself drifting off you had only to look at it and you woke up with a start. We ordered margaritas and talked, enjoying the river breeze which prevented us from melting clean away. A large catamaran (fascinatingly, this word also means a quarrelsome woman in Asian slang) was nestled into the lilies on the riverbank and men were trawling shrimp with little nets. You can reach this resort by sailing down the Saigon River in small boats but most people arrive in chauffeur-driven Mercedes. In the distance, I imagined I could hear someone singing Frank Sinatra classics with a Vietnamese accent: 'You're Just Too Good to be True', 'I've Got You Under My Skin'.

After a time of wonder, we moved up the garden to the restaurant where we were presented with the set menu. The food was underwhelming; I ate better on the street. It was also very long in coming. Someone had obviously told the fast-eating Vietnamese that foreigners like eating slowly and chatting a lot but the service was ridiculously unhurried. There was a grand piano on the stage and the reason for it soon became obvious when six Vietnamese gentlemen dressed in white pants and florid blue shirts moved into place with their instruments. The

Vietnamese can copy anything so there they were, singing and playing great renditions of jazz classics in almost perfect English. And who should leap onto the stage but party girl Françoise who had taken us to the one-dollar massage parlour in Saigon. She grabbed the microphone, all jumping breasts, tight pants and big smile, and began singing 'Days of Wine and Roses'. So I hadn't been dreaming after all. There she was singing Frankie, not only with an accent but flat.

I couldn't take my eyes off her. I couldn't believe she had the confidence to get up on a stage when she couldn't sing and that the musicians had the politeness to let her. They not only let her, they encouraged her as I found out later when she proudly played the CD she had recorded with them. Françoise would have been in her 40s (she had adult children), her eyes looked as though they had been surgically rounded and, like most people who have had drastic plastic surgery, she looked altered. Her breasts were spherical and hard and perfect and she didn't wear a bra. Actually a lot of upper-class Vietnamese women I met were altered, especially the faces. The Vietnamese adore sentimental, romantic songs and it was when Françoise sang in French that she came into her own. Her version of 'La Mer' was rather lovely as she sang in harmony (more or less) with the rotten-toothed saxophonist.

The restaurant by now was full of Europeans and wealthy Vietnamese with their children dressed in smocked frocks and pressed linen pants. In walked a smiling, relaxed, middle-aged man with a stunning, model-like, ponytailed young man. Alice greeted the man and he moved on to chat with the other tables. He looked famous.

'Who's he?' I asked her.

'That's Mr Khai Silk.'

'Really? And who's the beautiful boy with him?'

Alice gave one of her inscrutable, clouded looks. 'That is his (pause) friend.'

'Come on, Alice. He's married with a family. Would he really go out in public with what is apparantly his male lover?'

She got the inscrutable look again. They wandered off to lounge around in the pergola near the river. I decided there was a lot of things about Vietnamese society I hadn't yet been exposed to.

Françoise bounced over to our table and joined us to gorge on a durian or sau rieng fruit. It's soft and sticky with a rotten consistency and a faintly gamy putrid/honey taste. The smell, which comes from the skin, not the fruit, is like a teenage boy's bedroom distilled and blended with ammonia and diarrhoea. It looks like a melon with green spikes all over it. The women loved it to distraction and sucked out every last morsel of the pale lemon flesh. I lay back on the couch as far away from the durian as possible, accepted one of Alice's skinny French cigarettes and watched the storm threatening overhead in the languid tropical heat. Françoise, who is the sister-in-law of the owner, is the manager/maitre d' of Binh An. She seemed a woman of good heart and kind nature who hadn't quite understood a few things in life. At once vivacious and independent, tragic and lonely, she had been unlucky in love and was dancing as fast as she could to avoid the reality of her life — no talent, no man and good looks that the knife could only preserve for so long. This seems harsh but I say it only because it was what she herself thought would make her happy. Both she and Alice had lost great wealth and standing but they managed their changed circumstances very differently. I couldn't, however, fairly compare Françoise with Alice because the latter was a great natural beauty with enormous class. She was ageing gracefully as one would expect from a woman who was, for all her foibles, both intelligent and wise.

Back for a good night's sleep and writing in my 'day room' off the bedroom at the Continental. This is the set-up: furniture rearranged with two armchairs facing each other — one for my posterior and one for my swollen feet, side table equipped with gin and tonic, bottled water, tropical fruit, cellphone to call Ha when I spied her out the window and remote control for the air-conditioner. The trusty orange iBook was looking the worse for wear with cracks, the sound gone and cord held together with black masking tape. But this laptop had been through Moroccan deserts, damp French canal boats, the worst motel rooms television shoots can provide, jungles, tropical storms, Vietnamese electricity which is at best dodgy, and approximately 3000 kitchen benches. After I wrote the story of the love of my life on it, it had to be dismantled and dried out, so many tears had slid into the keys. It felt great to get the story out, a bit like being constipated for 20 years and finally discovering cascara. The publisher I showed it to judged it irredeemable and I've never wept into a laptop since. Every so often I got up and opened the window, letting in the throbbing metropolis, the rain and the heat. People who had stalls across the street outside the English bookshop had got used to my standing there so every time I showed, they waved and called.

I perused my research notes and realised I hadn't yet visited the famous Banh Xeo 46A restaurant. This is where doing a bit of reading up really pays off because this place is not in the central city and you would really have to know about it because there's a joint across the road that seems to have the same sign and food. This is common in Vietnam: in Hué, for example, there are three restaurants next to each other, all with almost the same name. The competition are obviously so used to everyone driving down the road and turning into the left and not the right that they practically do a three-act operetta to get you into their restaurant. You must be armed with knowledge and also with the tenacity to stick to your guns. The memory and sensation of that first banh xeo crepe I had tasted at the gastronomic fair in Can Tho helped my resolve. The taxi pulled up, a young man from the small Banh Xeo 46A ran over with an umbrella and a smile and escorted me up the three steps to my place. Long communal tables with red plastic stools were sheltered by a plastic awning, beer full of giant ice-cubes came immediately and I just sat there grinning with happiness, watching walls of water fall out of the sky like mirrored ribbons of silverfish.

The arrangement is the time-honoured Vietnamese one in which the business is an extension of their home out onto the footpath. Inside what is obviously the living room turned kitchen, women hover over great steaming pots, dozens of cooked chickens are lined up, a huge lump of pork sits on a bench and industrious chopping is going on everywhere. Outside seems to be boy department – large banana leaf baskets piled up with greens and herbs, spring onions, thinly sliced onions, bean sprouts, baskets of prawns, baskets of pork sliced into snippets and, most important of all, the pans for making the crepes. The cook squats over the hot oiled pan – about 25 centimetres across (this is not a small crepe) and throws in some onion and pork, swishes that around, then adds some halved prawns. Now the batter is poured over everything and swirled around, some bean sprouts are added, and after a bit more cooking the crepe is folded in half and served immediately. It sounds really simple but the secret is in the lightness of the crepe and the action of the hand in swirling the mixture very finely and evenly so it's like lace on the edges. From what I can work out, banh means cake or basically anything made with flour, and the word xeo is derived from the crackling sound as the crepe cooks.

The spanking hot crepe is placed in front of me along with a plate of greens and herbs which I put my face right into to get a hit of that aromatic perfume. This is where my joy and anticipation end. There are some very disagreeable things to be endured in Vietnam when you eat in the street. A legless man propels himself on a low trolley to sit right in front of me. He offers me his magazines but I don't want to buy any; I just want to eat my lunch. I offer him some of my food but he says no, smiling. He remains sitting there for my entire meal, staring at me, thus removing any possibility of enjoyment. Finally I can't stand it and change stools so I don't have to look at him. He moves so that he's in front of me again. I hate his life, I hate that he smiles through it, I hate myself for being so upset and angry, I hate the poverty, I hate that I feel guilty. As I leave I give him money and feel like either screaming or crying. Having ruined my meal he rolls on quietly to a young couple and sets up the vigil once more. They say no thank you, then ignore him. He will win.

Another really good cheap inside-outside restaurant is Bo Tung Xeo on Ly Tu Trong Street, not far from the Continental. The moment you enter this large place, you're hit in the olfactories by the smell of barbecueing meat. This is quickly followed by a stinging sensation in the salivary glands resulting in excess fluid in the oral cavity which can be relieved only by sitting down immediately and ordering the speciality of the house forthwith. The tables have green cloths and little cane lampshades, the chairs are white plastic, the high ceiling is made of flax basket lids and the entire place is suffused with smoke from the little braziers burning everywhere. Marinated beef strips and garlic cloves are cooked at the table by the chatty waiter who won't let you lift a finger. As it cooks, he delicately places the beef into your plate of rice, explaining the two dips – soy sauce and coconut cream – the peanut and chilli sauce, the greens, the current political situation, the weather in his home town. He signals the other waiters over, introduces you, tells them all about you and thanks you for loving his food so much.

The obvious enjoyment of food is something that is abhorred by some cultures and lauded by others. For Vietnamese to see a visitor sighing in pleasure over a meal means you love them, their culture, their fields, their animals and probably their family. But some individuals (Protestants, I should think) believe that people enjoying food in public is just one slippery move away from having sex in public. This is evidenced by a letter, reeking of repression, that I recently received from a man who had just watched my food show:

Peta Mathias
It's disgustingly bad manners the way you like to guzzle food down in front of viewers on TV. Perhaps you could try and refrain from making your appetite for food not quite so obvious.
Signed,
World War II veteran
Decorated
Weight Watched

One day, being tired of my own company, even though I'm not a World War II veteran, I applied lipstick, donned my raincoat, picked up my notebook and wandered over to the Duxton Hotel on Nguyen

Banh Gan
Vietnamese Crème Caramel

The main difference between French and Vietnamese crème caramel is the coconut milk. Some cooks put spices in the custard but most don't. I quite like it a little spiced. It tastes about a hundred times better made with fresh coconut milk.

Serves 8

115 g ($^1/_2$ cup) sugar

1 cup whole milk

2 cups fresh or tinned coconut milk

6 eggs

115 g ($^1/_2$ cup) sugar

half a vanilla pod or 1 tsp vanilla essence

1 star anise

3 cloves

8 half-cup ramekins

1   Make the caramel by boiling together $^1/_2$ cup of sugar with 4 tbsp water. The moment the sugar starts to become golden (takes about 7 minutes), whip it off the heat and pour into the ramekins. Tilt the ramekins to coat the entire bottoms with the caramel.

2   Preheat oven to 160°C (325°F). Make the custard by heating together the milk, coconut milk, vanilla (cut pod lengthwise and scrape out the grains with the back of a knife), star anise and cloves. Stir and when it is almost boiling, remove from the heat. Beat together the eggs and sugar and pour in the hot milk mixture, through a strainer. Stir well with a wooden spoon.

3   Ladle the custard into the ramekins and bake in a bain-marie for 35 minutes or until custards are just set.

4   Remove from the oven and leave the custards to cool. Chill well in the fridge.

To serve: Run a knife around the inside of the ramekins and turn the custards out onto plates, upside-down. You will be faced with perfect crèmes with the caramel on top, dripping down the sides.

Hué Bvd to visit somebody I knew would have no problems confusing different types of sensuality. He is young, handsome and smart. (I know what you're thinking but it was a coincidence that all my chef contacts in Vietnam were thus endowed.) There was just one hitch. He had forgotten about me. Lucky the lipstick was waterproof – it would last all day at a pinch. I sat in the lounge to wait and was led straight down the path of sin by tiered plates of vice with my name written on them. The best of these devil dainties were the lamingtons. The lamington of my childhood was a 5-centimetre square of shop-bought sponge cake, dipped in melted chocolate, then coated in finely grated coconut. Sometimes it was split in half and filled with whipped cream. It's probably an Australian invention (but don't tell New Zealanders that) named after a certain Lord Lamington, governor of New South Wales in the late 1800s. The lamingtons in front of me were about 3-centimetres square and the sponge had been layered with red jam, then dipped and coated in spiky coconut. They flew into the mouth like songbirds into a gilded cage. As the last drop of creamy Vietnamese coffee seeped through the filter, in walked Jon Bourbaud, perfect in his kitchen whites and fair hair. Executive chef, food and beverage manager of the flash Duxton, this was the man who would take me on my biggest adventure in Vietnam.

Like most grand hotel chefs, Jon has an exotic background of cooking all over the world. He is a New Zealander who trained in Melbourne then worked in the Savoy in London, then in the South-west of France which led to luxury yachts in Antibes. One of the yachts took him to Japan where his love affair with Asian food began. He worked in New Zealand for three years then in Brisbane at Ecco with the marvellous Philip Johnson. One day he felt like a challenge so went onto the Internet and found the job at the Duxton advertised. He studied Vietnamese for 10 months, cooks a mixture of Vietnamese and international food and knows all the best places to buy and eat. 'I'll pick you up from the Continental tonight at eight,' said he, disappearing into his huge kitchen and leaving me to contemplate the cream puffs.

Night falls early in Vietnam and it's always interesting to stand on the steps of the hotel and just watch. Asians, Brits and Australians wander in and out, as do a few Americans but not many. The 'parkers' are always very busy. For a small fee, they park your car or honda for you and guard it. Nobody in Saigon would ever just park any old place – you would never see your bike again. Hopeful cyclo drivers pedal laconically up and down, scouting for trade. The hotel porters chat and ask you what you've done with your day and how the book's going and have you put them in it. And then he's there, leaning out of the taxi shouting, 'I can't stop … too much traffic … get in.' Jon and I jump out at our destination and jump into the fabulous world of Com Nieu Saigon.

New Food Saigon is nothing short of amazing. The clean, white restaurant, divided in two on either side of the street is pumping, rice is flying, service is lightning fast, food is radiantly technicoloured and it's all overseen by the formidable Madame Ngoc. I got a glimpse of her before she disappeared off to her nightclub, incongruously well dressed and coiffed. Packets of chilled serviettes are popping all around us, breaking clay is shattering the occasional moments of calm and the waiters move around each other as if in a square dance. Jon, with the biggest smile on his face, peruses the huge menu and orders his favourites in Vietnamese. I peruse the menu and order anything outrageous in English – duck tongues, fried testicles or steamed womb with sour cabbage. The waiter looks at me and says the womb dishes are off. I'm devastated – now I'll never know what womb tastes like.

Canh thi la nau ngheu fennel and clam soup with tofu arrives, along with goi rau muong tom thit morning glory salad with shrimps and pork, muc hap hanh gung steamed squid with onion and ginger, ca tre chien nuoc mam gung fried catfish with ginger sauce, ca tim nuong thit bam grilled aubergine with chopped pork. We squeeze lime juice into a little bowl of salt and dive in. It is so hard to convey just how good this food is. It looks beautiful, tastes beautiful, is refined, not expensive and fresh beyond fresh. If you lived within walking distance of Com Nieu you would never cook again. Jon warns me to keep an eye out for the flying baked rice. Suddenly there's a shout, a waiter grabs a small clay pot of sizzling rice from the kitchen, whacks it with a hammer, shattering the pot all over the place, makes rapid eye contact with another waiter near our table and torpedoes the solid rice through the air. Our waiter catches it on a plate at the other end of the restaurant (they do this hundreds of times a night, the rice sometimes crossing paths like light aircraft in need of a traffic controller), tosses it up twice for added drama and lands it in front of us. Apparently they never drop it. He cuts the rice cake in four, throws chopped shallots, a dash of nuoc mam and salty sesame seeds over and leaves us to it. The outside is crispy and golden and the inside perfectly fluffy.

During the meal we discuss markets.

'What do you think is the best market in Saigon?'

'Where have you been?'

'Well, lots of street markets which seem to appear out of nowhere and of course Ben Thanh market with my little friend Ha.'

'What about Cholon?'

'I'm not really interested in Cholon because it's Chinese and I'm writing about Vietnamese.'

He looks at me long and hard.

'What?'

'I'm just wondering if I'll tell you about the night market or not because this place is bloody full on, probably dangerous and I'm not sure you could handle it.'

I bristle, as one does. 'Tell me or I'll kill you.'

'The night market is Saigon's wholesale market, open between midnight and 5 a.m. – only buyers go there. My buyers for the hotel shop there and occasionally I go on my motor scooter just for the experience but it's wild. You won't find it in any guidebook, you'll be the only white person and it's like nothing you've ever seen in your life – I can guarantee that.'

'Take me or you die.'

'Tonight?'

'Why not?'

'Okay. I'll pick you up at 2 a.m.'

'Yikes.'

'Be ready, wear rough clothes and don't bring money.'

I went back to the Continental, put on pants and a shirt which I tried to rough up, wrote a will, lay down, rewrote the will and went downstairs at 2 a.m. My mates, the hotel staff, were hanging around the door as usual, shirt necks loosened, shooting the shit. For once it wasn't raining. When they saw me their eyes widened.

'Good morning, madame. Where are you going, madame?'

'I'm going to the night market,' I said brightly.

They stared at me. 'What night market, madame? There is no night market.'

'Yes there is. My friend the chef is taking me. It's over there.' I pointed vaguely in the direction west of central Saigon.

They all looked rather concerned.

'Oh no, madame, you mustn't go to that market. That market not for ladies like you. Please go inside and go to bed.'

'I'll be fine. I'm a wild and crazy gal, you know. The lady thing is a cover.'

'Yes, madame. You very wild and crazy. You go back to bed.'

At that very moment, a fire-engine red 1952 Lambretta pulled up with a broadly smiling Jon at the helm and we sped off.

Driving through Saigon in the middle of the night was flabbergasting. Gone was the noise, gone were the crowds, gone was the mess and gone were the smells. Saigon really sleeps at night – the nightclubs supposedly close at midnight – and it's spotlessly clean and sparkling. Municipal cleaners come out like Cinderellas and sweep and flood the streets till they shine. We flew through the breezy, cool, quiet night like angels in the snow. Upon reaching the area around Nguyen Thai Hoc Street, we turned down and drove slowly into the edge of the huge, throbbing, outrageous night market, the source of every single spring onion, bitter melon or branch of coriander you eat in Saigon.

This is a world full of chicken feathers, not baskets but mountains of greens, the pungent smell of joss sticks and urine, kitchens set up in the street selling soups, sweet doughnuts and combination meals of rice or noodles and something else, children sleeping on the ground in the middle of it all, wild-looking women preparing vegetables and shelling beans. It has been raining, so it's sloshy and muddy underfoot but that doesn't bother the market people in their flimsy flip-flops; they just shuffle busily about in it. This isn't a relaxed market; this is a hard-working, hard-dealing, harsh market where business is business, men are men and women are nervous.

We slowly shunt deeper into the fantastic metropolis of food, moving gradually through the throngs, cyclos piled high with zucchini flowers, sweet potatoes and Chinese cabbage and the carts of buyers whizzing through the small space left on the street from the peasant sellers' produce spilling out from the footpath. Just think of any Asian market you've been to and quadruple it. We get the usual reaction — some of them know Jon, but my hair and the fact that I'm a foreign woman cause a sensation. Lots of people call out to us from doorways. We park the scooter down a side street and pay a woman nearby to look after it. She stares at us as if she's never seen Westerners before, then laughs and wishes us luck. Jon's natural politeness and ability with the lingo make me feel safe but I think it's a fantasy; I suspect, as we plough through, that things could turn against us at any moment. Every wide street, side road, alleyway, pavement, awning and secret tunnel is overflowing with primary produce of some description.

It's an underworld gastronomic *Bladerunner*, a giant medieval hippodrome on acid, a nocturnal Armageddon where the battle is not between good and evil but life and death. Peasants have travelled in from the countryside and if they don't sell the jack fruit, the family doesn't eat. We're like refugees from the day world; we have no business here as night-tripping spectators. Jon is very relaxed but I can't shut my mouth from astonishment. Back to the scooter and off to hit the fish section. Within five minutes of confronting an ocean of river and sea fish, we can no longer progress and have to backtrack. I get off the scooter to ease the congestion but then risk losing Jon altogether as we're pushed apart by the seething mass of hundreds of yelling people carrying thousands of fish on their backs, in boxes and in carts with an absolute commitment to anarchy and havoc. There's no point in trying to keep fish slime off me. I'm swimming upright, along with everyone else, in rivers of squid, flounder, prawns, frogs and crabs of every size and colour, carp, catfish, lobsters, sea bass, mackerel, scallops, clams, snails, giant tuna, cuttlefish, eels, red snapper. Eventually, laughing our heads off, we manage to get back together again, slide onto the scooter and wend our way out of the market. I pass a huge building full of food which says Cho Trai Cay Cau Ong Lanh which I think loosely means produce market.

'What time does the market finish?' I shout to Jon.

'At 5 a.m. they start packing up, the cleaners come in and by 8 a.m. there's absolutely no sign whatsoever that anything happened here. They're just normal streets with apartments and shops.'

'Unbelievable'.

'Had enough?'

'Yeah. But I'm desperate for a drink. I can't possibly go to bed without debriefing.'

'Okay. I know an all night café just around the corner from my hotel – we'll go there. Once again, we're talking rustic, Peta.'

'Just call me Indiana Jones.'

So here we are, seated on stools on the footpath at this roughneck joint, sipping cold lemon and soda and discussing the price of fish. The other customers are prostitutes, pimps, taxi drivers and night workers of various sorts, one of whom is playing a guitar and singing. A beautifully dressed vision from heaven appears in front of us.

'Hello. Would you like me to read your cards?' I blink at the little, middle-aged woman standing next to me.

'Have I gone troppo again? Am I suffering from post-traumatic stress hallucinations?' I ask Jon.

'No. This lady is well known around here. She spends the night wandering about reading people's cards.'

'At four in the morning.'

'At four in the morning.'

'Of course I'd like you to read my cards, madame,' I say, charmed.

She is perfectly coiffed, dressed and made-up (particularly good eyebrows) with jade and diamond earrings in her lobes and sparkly gold polish on her nails. In good English she tells me I have a lot of anger, am very honest, keep good health and will continue to do so and make huge money on property deals. I'm very interested to hear this as I'm a writer with no property. So now I'm an angry person with great assets I have no interest in but at least I'm honest. She then reads Jon's palm and it turns out he's trusting, not married and will also be a property tycoon.

'Why do you work at night?' I ask her.

'Because I like it, it's quiet and I don't sleep anyway.'

'Do you find it easier to sleep during the day?'

'Oh no. I have a full-time day job – I work in a clothing shop.' She smiles gently and moves off.

The quiet of the night is shattered by loud shouting. A couple of tables down from us two guys, who have been calmly chatting and drinking, have got into a fight over a prostitute. Suddenly one jumps to his feet, grabs a bottle and smashes it over his friend's head, following it up with a chair. The girl screams and starts tearing her long hair and the victim staggers out onto the road, a look of complete surprise on his white face and blood pouring from his head. He holds his head and stands, wavering, in the middle of the road in front of us.

'Christ,' says Jon, 'let's get out of here.'

'Shit,' I say, 'life is very exciting with you.'

As we leave, a taxi turns up and the injured man and a friend fall into it and speed away. By this time it's getting on for 4.30 a.m. and we drive past kids who are already playing football and tennis in the parks and wide streets in the dark.

'What are they doing up at this hour?'

'Everyone knows that this is the best time to play football – it's the only time there's space.'

Some children are sleeping on mats on footpaths and a few night owls wander in the pre-dawn tranquillity. When I get back to the hotel, there's no one to be seen – they're probably all out on a search party for me.

In my lurid dreams I sleep on a slippery sea of fish which undulates like a water bed, people wander around with blood pouring out of their heads and everyone is laughing at me. Jon is a tall, blond angel with blue eyes and his palms turned upward waiting to be read. I awake, sweating, to my last day in Vietnam thinking I'm lucky to be alive. In retrospect, I would go to the night market again because there are some things you have to do, but the more I reflect, the more I realise how dangerous it was and how naive I had been. The night market is like the dark side of Vietnam, like a giant jungle spiderweb catching juicy prey – not deliberately, but if you're in the way, the spider only does what comes naturally. I think of the story of the cricket who asked the poisonous spider to take him across the river on his back. The spider said, 'But aren't you afraid I would bite you?' 'No,' said the cricket, 'you know me, I'm your friend and you wouldn't harm me.' 'Okay,' said the spider, 'I'll take you across.' Halfway across the river the cricket felt the most agonising pain and realised the spider had bitten him. 'Why did you do it?' he gasped. 'Because it's in my nature and beyond my control,' replied the spider. At the same time the experience of the night market goes straight to the heart of the power of food in the lives of Vietnamese people – life, death, joy, misery, culture, family and endurance.

Epilogue

Vietnam is a place you can't wait to get out of and as soon as you've left, you long for the moment you can return. The heat and noise and dirt and poverty wear you down but they're all negated by the shockingly good food, witty, engaging people, breathtaking scenery and exotic architecture with that je ne sais quoi French influence. The Vietnamese have an extraordinarily high literacy rate. They read wherever they can, quote you poetry, describe ordinary events in sublime language and see beauty in everyday things. Despite the French influence, they still prefer Vietnamese food. They love pork paté, baguettes, coffee, beer and ice cream and say no thank you to the rest. They quietly 'follow their path' in every area of their lives.

At the airport I watch my last Vietnamese coffee drip into the cup with sweetened condensed milk in the bottom. I sip my last pho, this meal that symbolises Vietnam and her terrible history, this soup that can be anything you want but never changes its basic character. The Mongols introduced it, the French refined it, the southern Vietnamese improved on it, but it still retains its essential northern character – nourishing, tasty, beautiful to look at and ancient. And in Saigon I had found the pho of my dreams at Pho Hoa restaurant, so I was taking leave of Vietnam, happiness fulfilled, my senses imbued with the perfume of limes, coriander and fish sauce.

As I wait to board my plane to Hong Kong, Vietnamese moments fly through my mind – eating sweet mangoes, tasting my first pho, watching fish and chickens meeting their maker in the market, eating Chinese foie gras and noodle pillows, sleeping with jasmine flowers, munching on banana leaves, sipping sugar cane and rainbow drinks, falling in love with rice noodles, nibbling on French pastries, making Indochine gin and tonic, crunching happy crepes. The list seemed endless and everything unique and balanced – dew drop tea, white roses, good French wine, green papaya salad, crackly silkworms, yoke food, crab and asparagus soup, baguettes, roasted mouse, carry snacked, fresh rice paper rolls, international breakfast at the Rex, Phu Quoc nuoc mam, Vietnamese yoghurt, congee, flying rice, sour tamarind and acid lime. How can I live without this clean, tangy, healthy food?

The answer is, I can't. For better or for worse, the Vietnamese experience doesn't leave you unmoved. The people and the food contribute to your life in a way that is irrevocable, that enriches and ennobles your superficial pursuits, that balances you with its yin and yang. If you can say that food is love, then the Vietnamese are overflowing with it.

Index

This index lists food items, recipes, restaurants and markets. Page numbers for the main recipes are printed in bold type.